PRAYER STORM

DAILY PRAYER GUIDE

ENLARGED IN LOVE & HOLINESS

MARCH – APRIL 2026

Godson T. Nembo

ENLARGED IN LOVE & HOLINESS

Published in Cameroon by:
Christian Restoration Network
crnprayerstorm@gmail.com,
prayerstorm@christianrestorationnetwork.org

ISBN: 978-1-63603-343-3

All scripture quotations are from the New King James Version (NKJV) of the Bible except otherwise stated.

CONTACT

P.O. Box 31339 Biyem-assi, Yaounde, Cameroon
Tel.: 679.46.57.17, 652.38.26.93 or 696.56.58.64
Email: **godsonnembo@gmail.com** or
contact@christianrestorationnetwork.org
www.christianrestorationnetwork.org

WHERE TO BUY THIS PRAYER GUIDE:
SEE THE LAST PAGE

YOU CAN ACCESS ALL PRINTED HARD COPIES OF OUR BOOKS FOR ANY SPECIFIED

DURATION AT YOUR DOORSTEP.
Contact (237) 679465717 for subscription and payment details.

Prayer Storm Online Store: With MTN or Orange Mobile Money *(for those in Cameroon)* and E-Wallet *(for those abroad)*, you can easily obtain the electronic version of this book and other CRN publications via **www.amazon.com** at **https://shorturl.at/pqxyT** or **www.christianrestorationnetwork.org/our-bookstore** or **https://goo.gl/ktf3rT**

Printed in Yaounde, Cameroon by Mama press: (237) 677581523

TESTIMONIES:
Your testimony is a weapon against the kingdom of darkness. It is also a seed for someone else's miracle. Share with us what God has used this prayer guide and our books to do in your life; by SMS, telephone call or email.

BECOME A MINISTRY PARTNER:
Call the numbers: (237) 679.46.57.17 or 652.38.26.93 or 696.56.58.64 or send an email to:
crnprayerstorm@gmail.com or
contact@christianrestorationnetwork.org

Send your financial seed to:

- ECOBANK Acc. N°: **0040812604565101**
- Carmel Cooperative Credit Union Ltd. Bamenda Acc. N°: **261**
- ORANGE Mobile Money Acc. N°: **699902618**

- MTN Mobile Money Acc. N°: **674495895**

A NEED FOR DISTRIBUTORS:

If you are interested in the distribution of this Prayer Storm Daily Prayer Guide, call or send an SMS to any of these numbers for negotiations: (237) 675.68.60.05 or 677.43.69.64 or 652.38.26.93 or 696.56.58.64 or send an email to: **crnprayerstorm@gmail.com** (see last page).

TABLE OF CONTENTS

IMPORTANT EVENTS/ANNOUNCEMENTS

SPECIAL PRAYER PROGRAM		
RESTORATION PRAYER CAMP 10th Edition	**Venue**	**Date**
	Yaounde, Cameroon. Prepare to take part	**From Thu. 6th to Sat. 8th August 2026**
Contact WhatsApp: (237) 681722404 or 679465717/ Call: (237) 695722340 or 652382693.		

SPECIAL PRAYER STORM PROGRAM			
5 NIGHTS OF POWER WITH PASTOR GODSON	**Theme**	**Date**	**Join us daily at midnight (GMT +1) on YouTube, Facebook**
	RECOVER ALL	*From Friday 1st to Tuesday 5th May 2026*	

SPECIAL PROGRAM: I PRAY FOR YOU
Join Pastor Godson for a half hour morning devotion **every MONDAY, WEDNESDAY, and FRIDAY** from **6am** live on Facebook, YouTube **@PastorGodsonNemboTangumonkem**

HOUR OF RESTORATION
Join Pastor Godson & Anna TANGUMONKEM for HOUR OF RESTORATION **every TUESDAY** morning from **6 – 7:30am** in the banquet hall: Salle des fêtes « Fontaine de grâce » at Jouvence, Mendong street – Yaounde, Cameroon.. *A time of prophetic intercession for individuals, families and the nations.*

ANNOUNCEMENTS

- Festival of Fire series No. 1-5 and Power Must Change Hands Vol. 1-10 now available at XAF 3,000. Send your orders from today.
- Annual subscription to the Daily Prayer Guide from XAF 10,000 for electronic copies.
- All our books are available at our CRN Head office: 1st Floor Storey Building at Entrée Lycée de Tsinga village on the edge of the main road. **Contact:** 681.72.24.04, 695.72.23.40
- Carmel Credit Union, Yaoundé branch located at Carrefour Biyem-Assi, on the ground floor of the storey building, opposite Campus Crusade for Christ. **Contact:** +237 652.83.55.04
- Prayer Storm Bookshop at Cow Street Nkwen – Bamenda sells our books, Bibles and excellent Christian literature. **Contact:** 675.14.04.50, 674.59.35.98, 679.46.57.17.

"RESTORATION CAMP" Project

- The project for the establishment of the base for CRN in Yaounde, Cameroon began in January 2020.
- The LAYING OF THE FOUNDATION STONE FOR THE RESTORATION PRAYER HOUSE at Tsinga Village, Yaounde, took place in December 2023.
- For information on how to be part of the project, call or send SMS to **(237) 674.49.58.95, 678.16.46.88, 673.50.42.33, 699.90.26.18.**

Feedback Questionnaire:

We will love to hear your suggestions on how we can improve on this book: Send your comments to **(237) 681722404**, use the link https://prayer-stormdevotional.paperform.com/ or scan the QR CODE shown here to fill the online form.

HOW TO BECOME A CHILD OF GOD

Going to church and praying is not enough. *"Except a man is BORN AGAIN, he CANNOT SEE the kingdom of God." (John 3:3).*

The following steps will help you know how you can be born again.

Step 1: God Loves You and Offers a Wonderful Plan for Your Life

"For God so loved the world that He gave His only begotten Son, that whoever believes in Him should not perish but have everlasting life" (John 3:16). Jesus said, "*I came that they might have life and have it to the full." (John 10:10).*

No matter who you are and what you have done, God still loves you and wants to save you (Rom.5:8).

Step 2: Your Sins Have Separated You from God; That Is Why You Are Not Experiencing His Wonderful Plan for Your Life

"For all have sinned and fall short of the glory of God" (Rom.3:23)
"The wages of sin is death (spiritual separation from God) Rom.6:23.
All your religious activities and efforts cannot save you. God has provided a solution for you.

Step 3: Jesus Christ Is the Only Way Back to God

Jesus said, *"I am the way, the truth and the life, No one comes to the father except through me" (John 14:6).* Jesus is the only sacrifice God can accept for your sins. Through Him you can connect to God's plan for your life.

Step 4: You Must Personally Receive Jesus Christ as Your Saviour and Lord. Then You Can Know and Experience God's Plan for Your Life

Receive Him by personal invitation and by faith. *"Behold, I stand at the door and knock. If anyone hears My voice and opens the door (your heart), I will come in to him and dine with him, and he with Me." (Rev.3:20).*

If you are ready now to give your life to Jesus Christ, pray this prayer with all your heart.

"Dear Lord Jesus Christ, I need you. I open the door of my life and receive you as my Saviour and Lord. Forgive all my sins and wash me with your blood. Make me the kind of person you want me to be. Thank you for saving me."

Congrats! You are now a child of God.

Call us now let us pray for you: (237) 652.38.26.93 or 696.56.58.64

(Pastor Godson T. Nembo & Prayer Storm Team)

NOW THAT YOU ARE BORN AGAIN

Making the decision to become a born-again Christian, is the best decision you've ever made in your entire life and I congratulate you for that. The following points will help you enjoy your newfound life in Christ Jesus.

1. **Live with the Consciousness that You are Saved:** It is fundamental that you are certain of your new faith. This is referred to as the Assurance of Salvation. Believe that your sins have been forgiven and forgotten by God because of the price Jesus paid by His sacrificial death on the cross and that you are no longer under any condemnation (Acts 16:31, Rom.8:1-2, 2Cor.5:17, Jn.1:12).

2. **Join a Fellowship:** By new birth, you have entered the family of God. Locate a church that teaches and practises the scriptures truthfully, where the worship enables you to encounter God, and where the people are friendly and spiritual growth is encouraged (Heb.10:25, Gal.6:10).

3. **Get a Bible and Study It Daily:** You can begin from John, then Acts, Romans, etc. Just as a baby needs physical nourishment in order to grow, the Word of God is also the spiritual food by which we grow into Christlikeness (1Pet.2:2, Jn.5:24). Consult other mature Christians for any explanations.

4. **Commune Daily with God:** Through prayer, we talk with God, express our burdens to Him, as well as offer worship, praise and appreciation. We also have the privilege to get God speak to us, showering upon us His

love, peace, blessings and divine direction (Rom.10:9, 1Thess.5:17, 1Pet.5:8).

5. **Destroy Satan's Property in Your Keeping:** Desist from anything that does not glorify God. Do away with anything evil related to your sinful past, such as pornographic materials, stolen money and possessions, talismans, charms, juju, etc. (2Cor.6:17, Tit.2:11).

6. **Separate from Evil Friends and Get New Godly Friends:** Now that you are born again, you must discontinue the former way of life and walk in the truth (Ps.1:1-3, 2Cor.4:2; 5:17, Eph.4:22, 1Jn.1:6).

7. **Get Baptized:** Water baptism by immersion publicly authenticates our salvation and affirms our membership in the body of Christ (Rom.6:4, Col.2:12, Matt.28:19, Acts 2:38, 8:36).

8. **Seek the Baptism of the Holy Spirit:** The Holy Spirit assures us that we are saved and empowers us to live a holy life and do exploits for God through special gifts (Rom.8:14, Acts 2:1-4; 10:38, Eph.5:18).

9. **Tell Others about Jesus:** Our character should testify about our inner transformation. Also, our eagerness to tell others about God's love and lead them to Christ is also evidential about our salvation (Jn.4:28-29, Acts 4:10; 22:14, 2Tim.2:2).

10. **Worship God with Your Wealth through Offerings and Tithes:** Our cheerful giving is essential in advancing God's Kingdom – freewill offerings and tithe (one-tenth of our increase) (Deut.16:16-17, Prov.3:9-10, 2Cor:9:7).

11. **Make the Life of Christ Your Standard:** Fix your eyes on Jesus, the Author and Finisher of our faith Make Him your Role Model (Heb.12:2, Phil.2:5-11, Eph.4:24).

12. **Don't Abandon; Rise and Continue, if you Fall:** The Christian race may seem tough and challenging, with persecutions, distractions, oppositions, and even discouragements. But rest assured, you will make it by faith (Prov.24:16, Isa.41:10, Phil.1:6).

I pray that you will stand firm, and finish well like other heroes of faith, in Jesus' name! Amen.

Call us for counselling and prayer: (237) 652.38.26.93 or 696.56.58.64.

(Pastor Godson T. Nembo & Prayer Storm Team)

HOW TO USE THIS DAILY PRAYER GUIDE

I have discovered that some people do not know how to use this book well. As a result, they are not benefiting much from it. I will like to explain to you, how you can either use it during your personal prayer time or how to use it to lead a group prayer session.

Your Personal Prayer Time:

1. ***Read the topic of the day:*** It is the summary of the message of the day.
2. ***Read the Bible passages of the day aloud:*** You retain more, when you read aloud to yourself. In the early days, scriptures were read aloud.
3. ***Read the meditation slowly:*** Do it with a strong desire to understand.
4. ***Pray the prayer points:*** Read each prayer point and take time to pray well before you read the next one.
5. ***Pray for others:*** Use the prayer point to pray for other people as inspired by the Holy Spirit.
6. ***Add other prayer topics:*** For instance; dedicate your day, your family, your job, your Church, etc. to God.
7. Pray for your specific needs and those of others.
8. ***Action/Declaration:*** Take practical steps and do the prophetic declarations.
9. ***Prophetic Prayers of the Week:*** These prayers will be brought up every Monday. We encourage you to pray them every day during the week that follows.

Leading a Group to Pray:

1. Read the topic of the day aloud.
2. Assign one or more persons to read the Bible passage of the day aloud.

3. Read the meditation of the day aloud. After reading, you can make some comments, if necessary.
4. Allow other members of the group to make contributions or ask questions, if they have them.
5. Read one prayer point at a time. Then allow the people to pray for some time before you read the next one.
6. After they have prayed in chorus, you can ask one person to raise his/her voice and pray.
7. When you finish reading the prayer points, first ask the group members to give their own personal prayer plan.
8. At the end, let one person pray and conclude the session.

Bible Reading Plan:

We have included two Bible reading plans: **"Bible in 1 year"** and **"Bible in 2 years."** You can read through your Bible in one year by following the first plan in two years by following the second plan. Set aside time every day to read your Bible.

Read: 1 Peter 1:13-16

Bible in 1 year: Acts 13-14
Bible in 2 years: Exo. 17-18

"But just as he who called you is holy, so be holy in all you do; for it is written: 'Be holy, because I am holy'" (1 Peter 1:15-16 NIV).

Holiness is our calling and identity. The Greek word *'Hagios'* means "Set apart or consecrated." It is not just moral purity but separation unto God. When God calls us holy, He means we belong exclusively to Him.

In Christ, holiness is not optional; it is our destiny. Hebrews 12:14 declares, *"Without holiness no one will see the Lord."* To walk in holiness is to reflect God's nature in daily life. Jesus Christ is our model; He lived without sin yet reached out with compassion to sinners. Holiness, therefore, is not isolation from the world but living distinctly for God while influencing the world. Light is relevant only where there is darkness. You don't need a torchlight at midday. This sinful world needs holy men and women for healing and restoration.

Think of a clean glass of water placed in muddy surroundings. The water remains pure as long as it is not contaminated. Similarly, believers must remain pure while living in a corrupt society. We are "in the world but not of it" (John 17:16).

Holiness begins in the heart. Jesus said, *"Blessed are the pure in heart, for they shall see God" (Matthew 5:8).* It flows outward in our words, choices, and relationships. The Holy

Spirit empowers us to put off sinful habits and put on Christlike character (Ephesians 4:22-24).

Walking in holiness means guarding your thoughts, speech, and conduct, remembering you are God's temple. You were not redeemed with silver or gold but with the precious blood of Christ (1 Peter 1:18-19). Therefore, your life must glorify Him.

Action: *Is there any area of your life that makes you ashamed in God's presence? Decide to deal with it this month.*

Let us pray

1. *Father, thank You for calling me to a holy life in Christ, in Jesus' name.*
2. *Lord, cleanse my heart and mind from every hidden sin, in Jesus' name.*
3. *Holy Spirit, empower me to resist temptation daily, in Jesus' name.*
4. *Lord, let my life reflect Your purity and light in this dark world, in Jesus' name.*
5. *I declare that I am set apart, consecrated, and holy unto the Lord, in Jesus' name.*

Monday 2 March **STICK TO THE BLUEPRINT**

Read: 1 Corinthians 9:24-27

Bible in 1 year: Acts 15-17
Bible in 2 years: *Exo.19-20*

"And everyone who competes for the prize is temperate in all things. Now they do it to obtain a perishable crown, but we for an imperishable crown" (1 Corinthians 9:25).

God's Enlargement mandate is never fulfilled by excitement alone. Enlargement results from effectively executing a clear blueprint received from the Lord.

What is a "Blueprint?" It is a clear and intentional master plan that shows what to do, how to do it, and the order to follow, prepared in advance to guide the entire process of realizing a project. Every great realization begins with a vision from God that must be developed into a blueprint or roadmap.

The things God has revealed to you this year will never be materialized until you take action. That is why you must sit down and devise a clear plan of action to accomplish your vision.

Today, the Holy Spirit draws our attention to discipline – the inner strength that keeps you aligned when feelings fluctuate and pressure increases. Paul compares the Christian life to a race. Athletes do not train casually; they submit their appetites, time, and bodies to strict control because they want to win.

The word *"Temperate"* in today's verse comes from the Greek *'Egkrateia,'* meaning self-mastery, inner restraint, and power over one's desires. It is not weakness; it is controlled strength. Discipline is strength under direction.

We are not running the Christian race for applause, titles, or temporary rewards. We are running for an imperishable crown. We want our lives to become living platforms of the manifestation of God's glory. So, the great vision you have demands matching discipline. When your vision is large, but discipline is small, frustration is inevitable.

Isaiah 54:2 describes discipline as "Strengthening the stakes." Discipline strengthens your inner stakes so expansion does not collapse. Each time you say no to procrastination, comfort, or distraction, you are saying yes to destiny. Discipline protects your future from being traded for temporary relief.

I remember the story of a builder who ignored parts of an architectural plan to save time. The house went up quickly, but cracks appeared within months. When experts inspected it, they said, "The problem is not the foundation; it's that the builder didn't stick to the blueprint." Many believers pray for enlargement but modify God's plan to suit convenience. Enlargement lasts only as long as discipline preserves it.

God is not asking for perfection; He is asking for your consistency. Stick to the blueprint!

Action: *Choose one area where you lack discipline and practice intentional self-control there today as an act of obedience.*

Let us pray

1. *Father, uproot every form of laziness in my life and ignite in me a disciplined spirit to pursue my destiny diligently, in Jesus' name.*
2. *Lord, deliver me from procrastination and empower me to act promptly and faithfully according to Your blueprint for my life, in Jesus' name.*
3. *Father, release upon me the grace of self-control to govern my time, appetites, and choices so I may run my race lawfully and finish well, in Jesus' name.*
4. *Lord, strengthen my inner man with discipline and spiritual stamina so the enlargement You have ordained for me will stand firm and not collapse, in Jesus' name.*
5. *Father, I receive grace to pursue my God-ordained destiny with focus, consistency, and wholehearted commitment this year, in Jesus' name.*

Prophetic Prayers of the Week

1. ***"The LORD shall preserve you from all evil." (Psalm 121:7).*** *No evil will befall me this week, in Jesus' name.*
2. ***"With long life I will satisfy him." (Psalm 91:16).*** *Nothing will cut my life short. I will fulfill my days, in Jesus' name.*
3. ***"No weapon formed against you shall prosper." (Isaiah 54:17).*** *I overcome every satanic attack against my family and me today, in Jesus' name.*

Tuesday 3 March

GOD IS FAITHFUL, TRUST HIM

Read: Lamentations 3:22-23

Bible in 1 year: Acts 18-20
Bible in 2 years: Exo. 21

"God is faithful, by whom you were called into the fellowship of his Son, Jesus Christ our Lord" (1 Corinthians 1:9).

In a world marked by instability and betrayal, it is deeply reassuring to know that God is faithful. His faithfulness is not dependent on our goodness, strength, or even our belief. It is rooted in His unchanging character.

The word "faithful" in Hebrew is *'Emunah,'* and in Greek it is *'Pistos."* It conveys firmness, reliability, loyalty, and constancy. This means God is not just someone who occasionally does what He says; He is someone who never fails to do what He has promised. He is faithful by nature, not just by action. Think about it!

When life seems to contradict the Bible promises you know, when answers to your prayers are delayed, and you feel like giving up, don't worry about understanding what is happening to you; trust God's love for you. He is faithful! He cannot lie.

The prophet Jeremiah wrote Lamentations while mourning the destruction of Jerusalem. Yet in the middle of his grief, he declared, *"GREAT IS YOUR FAITHFULNESS."* That wasn't a feeling. That was a decision to trust God in his darkest hour. Can you still trust God after all you have gone through so far?

Jesus Christ is the greatest proof of God's faithfulness. Every prophecy about Him was fulfilled in Jesus. His birth (Isaiah 7:14), His death (Isaiah 53), and His resurrection (Psalm 16:10). These are not just stories; they are evidence that God keeps His Word, no matter how long it takes or how impossible it seems.

Imagine a farmer who plants seeds in barren soil. Day after day, he waters them though he sees no growth. Why? Because he believes that they will germinate. Likewise, you may not see the result of your prayers now, but God's faithfulness guarantees that His promises will manifest in your life in due time. Trust Him. He is faithful!

Action: *Are you trusting God for something? Write it down with at least two Bible promises concerning it, and then pray.*

Let us pray

1. *Father, thank You for Your constant and unfailing faithfulness in every season of my life.*
2. *Father, I place my confidence in Your promises, knowing You are not a man that You should lie.*
3. *O Lord, revive my heart in times of waiting, and remind me that You are always working.*
4. *Father, teach me to wait patiently, anchored in Your Word and not my emotions.*
5. *Father, help me keep my eyes on Christ, the living proof of Your covenant-keeping nature.*

Wednesday 4 March

DIVINE LOVE: THE EVIDENCE OF THE NEW BIRTH

Read: John 13:34-35

Bible in 1 year: Acts 21-23
Bible in 2 years: *Exo. 22-23*

"We know that we have passed from death to life, because we love the brethren. He who does not love his brother abides in death" (1 John 3:14).

Many people measure the new birth by outward signs – church attendance, prayer language, or religious activities. Yet Scripture gives a clearer and deeper proof of regeneration: **DIVINE LOVE.**

According to the apostle John, love is not optional for a believer; it is the unmistakable evidence that one has passed from spiritual death into life. You can't claim to be God's child but do not resemble your Father in love.

The love John speaks of is not mere human affection. It is *'Agape'* – the God-kind of love. *Agape* means unconditional, self-giving, and sacrificial love. It is love that seeks the good of others without demanding repayment. This love does not originate from human effort; it flows from God Himself. "God is love" (1 John 4:8), and when we are born again, His nature is imparted to us.

Jesus made this truth unmistakable. He said, *"By this all will know that you are My disciples, if you have love for one another" (John 13:35)*. Notice He did not say miracles, gifts, or titles would identify us. He said, LOVE. A believer may pray passionately and preach powerfully, yet if love is absent, the evidence of the new birth is questionable.

Divine love transforms relationships. It replaces hatred with compassion, pride with humility, and revenge with forgiveness. Saul the persecutor became Paul the apostle because the love of Christ invaded his heart. Likewise, when divine love fills a believer, old hostilities lose their grip.

Where love is absent, spiritual life is shallow. Where love flows, God's life is evident. The new birth does not merely change our destination; it changes our disposition. Love becomes our language, our response, and our testimony.

Beloved, the clearest proof that Christ lives in you is not what you say, but how you love people.

Action: *Ask the Holy Spirit to examine your heart and increase your capacity to love. Show love to someone who cannot pay you back this week.*

Let us pray

1. *Father, thank You for giving me new life through Christ, in Jesus' name.*
2. *Lord, fill my heart afresh with Your agape love, in Jesus' name.*
3. *O Father, remove every trace of hatred, bitterness, and unforgiveness from my heart, in Jesus' name.*
4. *Father, let my love for others be clear evidence of my new birth, in Jesus' name.*
5. *Merciful Father, help me love as Christ loved—sacrificially and sincerely, in Jesus' name.*

Thursday 5 March **A HEART OF COMPASSION**

Read: Matthew 9:35-38

Bible in 1 year: Acts 24-26
Bible in 2 years: *Exo. 24; 25:1-22*

"But when He saw the multitudes, He was moved with compassion for them, because they were weary and scattered, like sheep having no shepherd" (Matthew 9:36).

Jesus did not just see a crowd of people; He saw their pain, their exhaustion, and their spiritual hunger. The Bible says He was "moved with compassion." This means His love was not a passive feeling but a deep, gut-wrenching emotion that compelled Him to take action. To be enlarged in love is to move from being a spectator of human suffering to being a participant in the solution.

I remember a story of a young man who used to walk past a homeless beggar every morning on his way to work. For months, he simply tossed a coin and kept walking, feeling he had done his "duty." One day, the Holy Spirit prompted him to stop, look the man in the eye, and ask his name. That five-minute conversation revealed a broken soul who just needed to be seen as a human being. Compassion starts when we stop rushing and start seeing.

When we become desensitized to the suffering around us—whether it is poverty, sickness, or loneliness—we lose a part of our Christ-like nature. Holiness is often misconstrued as avoiding people to stay "clean," but true holiness involves getting your hands dirty to help the "weary and scattered." God is calling us in this season to have hearts that are easily moved by what moves Him.

Action: *Today, find one person who looks "weary" or "scattered"—a neighbor, a vendor, or a colleague—and offer them a word of genuine encouragement and a prayer.*

Let us pray

1. *Father, I thank You for the compassion You have lavished upon my life.*
2. *Lord, take away every heart of stone and give me a heart of flesh today.*
3. *Holy Spirit, sensitize my spirit to notice the "weary and scattered" in my path.*
4. *Father, give me the courage and resources to act on the compassion I feel.*
5. *Lord, let our church be known as a house of compassion for the broken-hearted.*

Friday 6 March **THE FRAGRANCE OF CONSECRATION**

Read: 2 Corinthians 2:14-17

Bible in 1 year: Acts 27-28
Bible in 2 years: *Exo. 25:23-40; 26:1-14*

"For we are to God the fragrance of Christ among those who are being saved and among those who are perishing" (2 Corinthians 2:15).

A famous story is told of a man who worked in a perfume factory. Every evening, when he walked home, he didn't have to tell anyone where he had been; the scent of the oils and essences clung to his clothes and skin so strongly that people could smell him from a distance. In the same way, holiness is a spiritual fragrance. When you spend time "shut in" with God, separated from the noise and pollutants of the world, you begin to carry an aroma that people can sense before you even open your mouth.

Consecration is the process of setting yourself apart specifically for God's use. It is the "enlargement" of your inner man so that the beauty of Christ can be seen through you. However, just as a beautiful perfume can be ruined by a few drops of sewage, our spiritual fragrance is easily spoiled by "dead flies" of compromise. Small acts of disobedience or a bitter attitude act like pollutants. People may not see your secret life, but they can "smell" the difference between a person who is truly consecrated and one who is merely religious.

If you want to be effective in winning souls, you must prioritize this fragrance. You don't need to argue the gospel as much as you need to "aroma" the gospel. When your character is holy, and your heart is pure, you become an attraction to those who are perishing. They will see your peace in a storm and your integrity in a crisis and ask, "What is that scent?" Today, determine to stay in the "perfume factory" of God's presence. Let the Holy Spirit rub the essence of Christ's character into your soul until you smell like Heaven.

Action: *Take 15 minutes of "quiet time" today with no phone or distractions. Simply sit in God's presence and ask Him to "re-perfume" your spirit for the day ahead.*

Let us pray

1. *Father, I thank You for the privilege of being a carrier of Your presence.*
2. *Lord, let the fragrance of my life be pleasing and sweet to You today.*
3. *O Lord, remove every "dead fly" of secret sin that is spoiling my testimony.*
4. *Father, help me to stay consecrated and set apart for Your holy use.*
5. *Holy Spirit, let the character of Jesus be so evident in me that it draws others to You.*

Saturday 7 March

INVEST THE LITTLE YOU HAVE

Read: Mark 4:24-33

Bible in 1 year: Joel 1-3
Bible in 2 years: *Exo. 26:15-37; 27*

"For whoever has, to him more will be given; but whoever does not have, even what he has will be taken away from him" (Mark 4:25).

God increases us in two powerful ways: He gives seeds to sow and releases rain for growth. Many people ask, *"What seed has God given me?"* Your life itself is a seed – your breath, time, talents, spiritual gifts, job, salary, ideas, and even what others give to you.

Note this: God supplies the seed, but you are responsible for sowing it if you desire enlargement. As John C. Maxwell wisely said, *"The ground always asks for your seed and not your need."* Needs are not conquered by wishes, but by intentional sowing and wise investment.

This principle explains Jesus' words: *"For whoever has, to him more will be given…" (Mark 4:25).* At first glance, it may seem unfair. Why should those who already have be given more? Jesus clarifies this truth in Matthew 25:29 (NLT): *"To those who use well what they are given, even more will be given, and they will have an abundance."* Increase is not about possession alone, but about stewardship. What you do with what God has placed in your hands determines what He adds next. Diligence is the key.

1. ***Diligence Produces Prosperity:*** Scripture says, *"The hand of the diligent makes rich" (Proverbs 10:4).* Genuine

prosperity is never accidental; it is the fruit of consistent effort.

2. ***Diligence produces leadership:*** Proverbs 12:24 says, *"The hand of the diligent will rule."* Slackness disqualifies, but diligence positions you for influence. Engage diligence to emerge this year
3. ***Diligence fuels creativity:*** Proverbs 21:5 says, *"The thoughts of the diligent tend only to plenteousness."* Creative solutions flow from committed minds.
4. ***Diligence Brings Promotion:*** Proverbs 22:29 says, *"Seest thou a man diligent in his business? he shall stand before kings; he shall not stand before mean men."* Your excellent work will open doors for you that no human connection can forcc.

What has God given you? Do not despise it. Diligently invest your seed while trusting God for the rain of increase.

Action: *Identify an area God wants you to invest in. Make a plan to start soon.*

Let us pray

1. *Thank God for all He has given you by His mercy and grace.*
2. *Father, deliver me from an ungrateful attitude and open my eyes to see the seeds You have given me, in Jesus' name.*
3. *Father, baptize me with grace to be diligent in all I do this year, in Jesus' name.*
4. *Fire of God, purge out laziness and nonchalance from my heart, and the hearts of my children, in Jesus' name.*
5. *Father, strengthen my hands to take my work to the level of excellence this year, in Jesus' name.*

Sunday 8 March **GOD'S WORD IS FINAL**

Read: *Isaiah 54:13-17*

Bible in 1 year: Amos 1-3
Bible in 2 years: Exo. 28

"God is not a man, that He should lie, nor a son of man, that He should change His mind. Does He speak and then not act? Does He promise and not fulfill?" (Numbers 23:19 NIV).

No man can change what God has said about you. Believe this eternal truth! The people of this world may engage manipulation, injustice, or demonic opposition against you. Wicked people may set up visible or invisible embargoes against you. They may use corrupt systems, twisted laws, and even spiritual forces to try to delay or destroy what God has ordained for you. But take heart: man's verdict is not God's final word. All their plans against you will fail, in Jesus' name.

In Numbers 23:20, Prophet Balaam, hired to curse Israel, declared, *"He has blessed, and I cannot reverse it."* The Hebrew word for "Reverse" here implies to *undo, cancel, or make void.* Once God commands a blessing, no force can revoke it. His Word is unchallengeable in every court, natural or spiritual.

The Bible gives clear examples of people using God's Word and divine alignment to overturn evil decrees. In Esther 8, Haman's wicked law was set to destroy the Jews. But Esther, through fasting and boldness, moved the king to issue another decree that gave God's people the right to fight back. In Daniel 6, a law was passed forbidding prayer, but

Daniel chose God over compromise, and God overruled that decree by delivering him from the lions' den.

The Word of God is your legal authority to overturn every negative word, curse, or manipulation. Isaiah 54:17 affirms, *"No weapon formed against you shall prosper, and every tongue that rises against you in judgment, you shall condemn."* This is not wishful thinking; it is covenant language.

Imagine a seal on a royal decree. Once stamped, only the king can change it. God's stamp is on your destiny; that is why no one else holds the authority to reverse it. You are blessed! No one can curse. Don't surrender to Satan's lies. It shall be well with you, in Jesus' name.

Action: *Identify any negative thoughts harassing you and continuously cancel them with the blood of Jesus and the Word during the next seven days.*

Let us pray

1. *Father, thank You because Your Word over my life is final and irreversible.*
2. *Father, empower me to stand on Your promises when the world speaks otherwise, in Jesus' name.*
3. *Father, help me detect and reject every evil decree spoken against me, in Jesus' name.*
4. *Lord, let my life align with Your voice and not the lies of the enemy, in Jesus' name.*
5. *I decree that every contrary voice and wicked law working against my life is cancelled by the power of the Word and the blood, in Jesus' name.*

Monday 9 March **TIME TO BREAKTHROUGH**

Read: Luke 5:1-10

Bible in 1 year: Amos 4-6
Bible in 2 years: *Exo. 29*

"And when they had done this, they caught a great number of fish, and their net was breaking" (Luke 5:6).

Do you feel stuck – defeated by resistance, opposition, or stagnation? Are you thinking that nothing works for you and that a heavy hand is standing in the way of your progress? But the God we serve is the God of breakthroughs. As He did for Peter, He is able to turn emptiness into abundance in one moment of obedience.

"*Breakthrough*" in Hebrew is *'Perets,'* meaning "Bursting forth, breaking out, or advancing beyond barriers." It speaks of God's intervention that shatters limitations and opens new possibilities.

Breakthrough begins with desire – A CONVICTION THAT CHANGE IS POSSIBLE. Peter longed for a catch despite failure. Without desire, you settle in defeat. Yet your desire must be matched **with** determination. Peter toiled all night without quitting. Determination breaks resistance. Proverb 10:4 says, *"The diligent hand brings wealth."*

Jesus then called him to DEVELOP – to go deeper. Friend, shallow effort produces shallow results. Breakthrough requires growth in your skills, prayer, and faith. Next, Peter had to do what Jesus commanded: *"Launch out into the deep and let down your nets."* Desire alone does not birth miracles; obedience does.

Breakthrough also requires us to deal with opposing forces. Life often presents spiritual resistance, which we must overcome through fasting, persistent prayer, and the declaration of God's Word.

Then we must dwell in God's presence. Peter offered his boat for Jesus' ministry. Remaining close to Christ creates the atmosphere for divine intervention.

Finally, a breakthrough helps us discover purpose. Peter's miracle catch pointed him to a greater calling: *"From now on you will catch men" (Luke 5:10).* True breakthrough is not just about money or success; it's about aligning with God's mission.

Your failure is not final. God is stepping in this season, and your night of emptiness will become a morning of overflow. Like Peter, you will move from frustration into destiny.

Action: *Take time today and ask God to show you what you must do for your breakthrough.*

Let us pray

1. *Father, thank You because You are the God of breakthroughs, in Jesus' name.*
2. *Lord, give me fresh desire and determination to pursue the change You have for me, in Jesus' name.*
3. *Father, take me deeper in prayer, wisdom, and skill to unlock new levels, in Jesus' name.*
4. *Father, teach me to obey Your instructions fully, no matter how simple they seem, in Jesus' name.*
5. *I declare: My night of emptiness is over – I walk into breakthrough and divine purpose, in Jesus' name.*

Prophetic Prayers of the Week

1. ***"He shall direct your paths." (Proverbs 3:6).*** *Today, **I** am delivered from costly errors and wrong decisions, in Jesus' name.*
2. ***"I am the LORD who heals you." (Exodus 15:26).*** *Today, **I** receive divine health and strength, in Jesus' name.*
3. ***"The LORD will keep you from all harm." (Psalm 121:7).*** *Today, my family and I are preserved from accidents and disasters, in Jesus' name.*

Tuesday 10 March

CONFRONT REBELLION IN YOUR HEART

Read: Jeremiah 43:1-7

Bible in 1 year: Amos 7-9, Oba. 1
Bible in 2 years: *Exo. 30*

"My son, give me your heart, and let your eyes observe my ways" (Proverbs 23:26).

Rebellion always begins in the heart quietly, long before it becomes visible in your words and actions. Is there rebellion in your heart?

"Rebellion" is the deliberate resistance of the heart and will against God's authority, expressed through stubborn disobedience to His Word, even when His will is clearly known. In Jeremiah 43, God spoke clearly through His prophet, instructing the people to remain in Judah. Instead of yielding, Azariah, Johanan, and the others accused Jeremiah of lying. Their problem was not confusion; it was pride. They heard God's Word, understood it, and deliberately rebelled against it.

Rebellion is first a heart posture, not merely an action. It is the inward decision to oppose God's rule while still wanting His protection. Rebellion says, "I know what God said, but I prefer my way." "I don't want anybody to tell me what to do."

At the root of rebellion is pride. Pride distorts judgment, making us feel wiser than God and defensive when corrected. It pushes us to shift blame, question spiritual authority, and justify disobedience. This is exactly what happened in Jeremiah's day. Instead of repenting, the people became bold in error. Scripture warns us that pride always ends in destruction (Proverbs 16:18).

Rebellion is not always dramatic. Often it hides in delayed obedience, selective submission, and silent resistance. Jonah did not shout against God; he simply ran away, and the storm followed him. Saul did not openly reject God; he partially obeyed and lost his kingdom. God's verdict was clear: rebellion is as serious as witchcraft because both replace God's authority with self-will (1 Samuel 15:23).

The cure for rebellion is humility. A humble heart trembles at God's Word, even when it confronts comfort, plans, or emotions. When we invite the Holy Spirit to search us, He exposes hidden resistance and heals it. Freedom is not found in resisting God, but in surrendering fully to Him.

Rebellion tolerated today will damage tomorrow. Confront it early.

Action: *Ask the Holy Spirit to reveal any area of rebellion in your heart and obey Him promptly today.*

Let us pray

1. *Father, thank You for warning me in love whenever rebellion rises in my heart, in Jesus' name.*
2. *Lord, expose every hidden pride and stubbornness in me, in Jesus' name.*
3. *O Father, deliver me from selective obedience and teach me to fully submit to Your Word, in Jesus' name.*
4. *Father, break every cycle of accusation and finger-pointing in my life, in Jesus' name.*
5. *Father, give me a humble and teachable spirit that treasures Your counsel, in Jesus' name.*

Read: Ephesians 3:17-21

Bible in 1 year: Jonah 1-4
Bible in 2 years: *Exo. 31-32*

"But above all these things put on love, which is the bond of perfection" (Colossians 3:14).

Do you want to experience God's grace for enlargement? JUST LOVE PEOPLE. Wear love as a garment. Be perfumed with God's love everywhere you go. It is the secret to attract God's favor.

Christianity without love is like a painted fire that cannot burn – it doesn't impact the world. People are attracted to Jesus Christ when we consistently manifest God's love to them. We have seen already that God's love is "Agape love," also described in the Bible as charity.

Most people love others when they have a good reason to do so. It is natural to love those who have shown you kindness. In fact, they become your friends. You don't need to pray and fast to love someone who gives you monthly money or speaks well about you to everybody. We readily give to those who have given to us. Some people find it challenging to give to those who cannot repay them. It takes God's love to be kind to those who hate, criticize, and castigate you.

Beloved in Christ, you must aim at cultivating the God-kind of love. Paul describes it in our main verse as *"The bond of perfection."* He is saying that divine love binds us together in perfect unity. If something keeps pulling you away from the fellowship of believers, it is a sign that you are not living in God's love. Often, to break away from fellowship, people who lack God's love try to hide behind revelations and prophecies.

1 Corinthians 13:8 says, *"Love never fails!"* God is love, and He never fails. So, if you love like Him, you cannot fail. In our society, some people are abandoned in their old age because they sowed few seeds of love in their youth. If you neglect your children today, you may suffer rejection in the future. So, now that you are young and robust, invest in as many people as possible. God will pay you back when you need it.

Ephesians 3:17 says, *"Christ may dwell in your hearts through faith; that you, being rooted and GROUNDED IN LOVE" (Ephesians 3:17).* The foundation of God's Kingdom is love. Be rooted in God's love by just loving everybody – the best, the good, the bad, and the ugly.

Action: *Identify someone you would not naturally show love to, and intentionally do something kind for them within the next week.*

Let us pray

1. *Father, thank You for calling me into the Kingdom of love, in Jesus' name.*
2. *Father, I choose to live a life of love by loving everybody; give me grace, in Jesus' name.*
3. *Place your hand on your heart and pray 5 times, "I receive grace to love the lovable and the unlovable, in Jesus' name."*
4. *Father, deal in my heart any attitude that kills love and collaboration with others, in Jesus' name.*
5. *Father, give me the grace to conquer evil with good and not the contrary, in Jesus' name.*

Thursday 12 March **THE UNSTAINED GARMENT**

Read: Ecclesiastes 9:7-10

Bible in 1 year: Hos. 1-4
Bible in 2 years: *Exo. 33-34*

"Let your garments be always white, and let your head lack no oil." (Ecclesiastes 9:8)

Imagine you are wearing a brand-new, pure white suit to a wedding. You would be incredibly mindful of where you sit, who you hug, and how close you stand to the buffet. You wouldn't be "legalistic" or "cranky"; you would simply be protective of your appearance because you value the garment. Holiness is very much like that white suit. It is a spiritual garment given to us by grace, but the Bible holds us responsible for keeping it white in a world full of "muddy" influences.

In the Bible, Joshua the High Priest stood before God in filthy rags until the Lord commanded, *"Take away the filthy garments from him."* God is the one who provides the white robe of righteousness, but we are the ones who must decide where we walk. You cannot frequent environments of gossip, malice, or compromise and expect your garment to stay white. Small stains—a "little" lie here, a "small" grudge there—eventually dull the radiance of your spiritual life until the "oil" of the Holy Spirit no longer flows freely.

To be enlarged in holiness, you must develop a healthy "sensitivity to stains." This isn't about living in fear; it's about living in love for the One who clothed you. When you value your walk with God, you naturally avoid things that smudge your conscience.

If you do happen to slip and get a stain, don't wait until Sunday to deal with it. Run to the blood of Jesus immediately for cleansing. Keep your garments white, and you will find that the oil of favor and authority will never be lacking on your head.

Action: *Today, identify one grey area in your life, such as a habit or a conversation style that tends to stain your peace, and decide to lay it aside.*

Let us pray

1. *Father, I thank You for clothing me in Your garment of righteousness.*
2. *Lord, give me a sensitive heart that quickly recognizes the "stains" of sin.*
3. *O Lord, I receive the grace to walk away from environments that soil my spirit.*
4. *Father, let the fire of the Holy Spirit consume every hidden impurity in my life.*
5. *Holy Spirit, let Your oil stay fresh upon my head as I walk in purity today.*

Friday 13 March

THE REFINER'S FIRE

Read: Malachi 3:1-4

Bible in 1 year: Hos. 5-7
Bible in 2 years: *Exo. 35*

"He will sit as a refiner and a purifier of silver; He will purify the sons of Levi, and purge them as gold and silver" (Malachi 3:3)

In the ancient process of refining silver, the refiner would sit in front of a furnace, holding the metal in the hottest part of the flame. This was done to burn away the "dross", the impurities that make the metal dull and brittle. How did the refiner know when the process was complete? He knew the silver was pure when he could look into the molten metal and see his own reflection clearly. This is exactly what God is doing in your life. Holiness is not God trying to punish you; it is God trying to get the dross out so He can see His reflection in you.

Often, we pray for "enlargement" and "elevation," but we shy away from the heat of the Refiner. The heat comes in the form of divine corrections, the convictions of the Holy Spirit, or the challenging seasons that test our integrity. When you are tempted to lose your temper, but the Holy Spirit whispers, "Be patient," that is the heat of the furnace. When you are tempted to take a shortcut with money, but you choose the long road of honesty, a little more dross is burned away. God is not interested in just making you "shine"; He is interested in making you pure.

Gold is more valuable than iron because it has been through more heat. If you want to carry the heavy weight of

God's glory, you must be willing to let the fire consume your pride, your lust, and your secret dependencies. Don't run from the fire of God's Word. Embrace it, for on the other side of that furnace is a version of you that looks just like the Master, Jesus Christ.

Action*: Today, pay close attention to your impulses. The moment you feel a surge of pride or irritation, stop and say, "Lord, let Your fire consume this dross," and choose a holy response instead.*

Let us pray

1. *Father, I thank You because You love me enough to refine and purify my soul, in Jesus' name.*
2. *Lord, let Your fire consume every "dross" of sin and pride in my heart today, in Jesus' name.*
3. *Lord, give me the grace to endure the heat of Your correction without complaining, in Jesus' name.*
4. *Father, let my life become a clear reflection of the character of Jesus Christ, in Jesus' name.*
5. *Holy Spirit, purge my thoughts and motives until they are transparent before You, in Jesus' name.*

Saturday 14 March

LEAVE WELL TO START WELL

Read: Genesis 13:8-11

Bible in 1 year: Hos. 8-10
Bible in 2 years: *Exo. 36*

"Blessed are the peacemakers, for they shall be called sons of God" (Matthew 5:9).

Life runs in seasons. In a new season, God may lead you to separate from a place of employment or leadership in order to begin something new for yourself. It is not a sin if God is the author of the new idea.

In Genesis 13, Abram and Lot faced growth-related tension. Instead of allowing conflict to corrupt their relationship, Abram chose peace, honor, and trust in God. He did not grasp, compete, or manipulate his nephew. He left room for God to enlarge him in His own way.

Biblical separation is never rooted in offense, pride, or rebellion. It flows from divine direction and is carried out with integrity. David refused to harm Saul even when Saul stood in the way of his promotion. Joseph did not force his way out of prison; God promoted him in due time. Scripture consistently shows that God blesses transitions that are clean, peaceful, and honorable.

Leaving well matters because how you exit determines how you enter the blessing in your next season. When separation is done dishonestly, through gossip, theft of ideas, or secret schemes, it pollutes the future. But when it is done with humility, transparency, and excellence, God Himself becomes the defender and promoter.

A ripe fruit separates naturally from the tree without tearing the branch. It falls because it is ready, not because it is bitter. In the same way, godly separation happens when a season is fulfilled, not when hearts are wounded.

When God is leading you to start your own work, He calls you to finish faithfully, honor authority, and trust Him for increase. Clean hands attract divine backing.

Action: *Have you received a burden from God to leave where you are serving now to start something new? Pray and seek counsel for wisdom to do it correctly.*

Let us pray

1. *Father, I thank You for the season, people, and opportunities You have used to prepare me, in Jesus' name.*
2. *Lord, purify my motives and deliver me from pride, offense, and bitterness in every transition, in Jesus' name.*
3. *Grant me wisdom to separate only by Your direction and not by emotion or pressure, in Jesus' name.*
4. *Father, help me to honor authority and finish every assignment faithfully and excellently, in Jesus' name.*
5. *Father, cause me to enjoy the fruit of my labor this year, in Jesus' name.*

Sunday 15 March **LOVE BELIEVES THE BEST**

Read: 1 Corinthians 13:1-7

Bible in 1 year: Hos. 11-14
Bible in 2 years: *Exo. 37-38*

"Love... bears all things, believes all things, hopes all things, endures all things." (1 Corinthians 13:7)

One of the most powerful characteristics of God's love is its ability to believe the best about people. In a world full of cynicism and suspicion, love chooses to express faith in the possibility of change and growth in others. When you love someone, you don't just see them as they are; you see them as they can become in the hands of God. This positive expectation is what often triggers the transformation we desire to see.

Do not give up on your relationships, even when they are going through a difficult season. Whether it is a rebellious child or a spouse who seems cold, love continues to hope and expect the best. This kind of love is not a human product; it requires the supernatural help of the Holy Spirit. As Romans 5:5 says, God's love is poured into our hearts by the Spirit. When your own strength fails, tap into the reservoir of divine love.

If you want to see transformation in your home or workplace, start by changing the way you see and speak about people. Replace criticism with hope. When you believe the best about someone, you are creating an environment where they can flourish. Ask God for a fresh outpouring of His love today so that you can reflect His heart to everyone you meet.

Action: *Identify one person you have been critical of and find one good* *thing to say to them or about them today.*

Let us pray

1. *Father, thank You for believing the best about me even when I fail.*
2. *Lord, heal my heart from every hurt that makes me suspicious of others.*
3. *O Lord, give me the grace to believe in the potential of those around me.*
4. *Father, let Your love in me be stronger than any disappointment I face.*
5. *Lord, use my words of hope to encourage someone who is on the verge of quitting.*

Monday 16 March **GIVING A SECOND CHANCE**

Read: Luke 15:11-32

Bible in 1 year: Mic. 1-3
Bible in 2 years: *Exo. 39*

"Be kind and merciful, and forgive others, just as God forgave you because of Christ." (Ephesians 4:32)

Mercy is not just about helping the poor; it is also about giving people a second chance. When someone hurts us, our natural reaction is to want to pay them back or write them off completely. However, the wisdom from above is full of mercy. The more we grow in God, the more patient we become with the weaknesses and mistakes of others. If God gave us a second chance, how can we deny it to those who offend us?

Consider the father of the prodigal son. He didn't wait for his son to finish his apology; he ran to him, embraced him, and restored him immediately. This is the heart of a person enlarged in love. Instead of being bitter or rude, we are called to be kind and merciful. Is there someone in your life you have "written off"? Today, God is asking you to extend the same grace He has extended to you.

Being merciful does not mean you approve of the sin, but it means you value the soul more than the offense. When we offer a second chance, we are reflecting the character of Christ, who prayed for His executioners. This week, choose to be the person who builds bridges instead of walls. Your mercy might be the very thing that brings that person to repentance.

Action: *Think of someone you have been harsh with lately and reach* *out to them with a word of kindness or an offer of a second chance.*

Let us pray

1. *Lord, thank You for the many second chances You have given me.*
2. *O Lord, help me to be kind and merciful to those who have failed me.*
3. *Father, remove every spirit of pride and self-righteousness from my heart.*
4. *Lord, give me a heart that values restoration more than retaliation.*
5. *Father, let Your mercy flow through me to touch someone who is struggling.*

Prophetic Prayers of the Week

1. **"You will find favor and good success." (Proverbs 3:4).** *God's favor will open uncommon doors for me today,* ***in*** *Jesus' name.*
2. **"Humble yourselves… that He may exalt you." (1 Peter 5:6).** *I receive divine promotion and lifting today, in Jesus' name.*
3. **"Surely goodness and mercy shall follow me." (Psalm 23:6).** *As I step out today, I am clothed with the garment of mercy and favor, in Jesus' name.*

Tuesday 17 March **THE TEST OF PROMOTION**

Read: Deuteronomy 8:11-14

Bible in 1 year: Mic. 4-7
Bible in 2 years: *Exo. 40*

"But he gives more grace. Therefore it says, "God opposes the proud but gives grace to the humbles" (James 4:6).

Do you know that promotion is both a blessing and a test? Many pray to be lifted, but few remain humble after God answers them.

Every promotion reveals what truly rules the heart. Scripture warns, *"When you have eaten and are full, beware lest you forget the Lord."* Success without humility becomes the seed of downfall. The higher God lifts you, the lower you must bow before Him.

Joseph ruled Egypt but never lost his tenderness toward God or people. Though powerful, he still wept with compassion and gave glory to God for every success. In contrast, King Saul started humble but allowed pride and disobedience to dethrone him. Promotion reveals character. What pressure exposes, power magnifies.

A young pastor once shared how his small ministry grew into a city-wide influence. At first, he served with humility, but after fame came, he began to ignore prayer and mentorship. Within a few years, scandals and conflicts brought him low. In tears, he later said, "I lost my crown when I lost my humility." God restores, but He resists the proud and gives grace to the humble.

Humility is not weakness; it is strength under control. It recognizes that every achievement is a gift of grace. True humility doesn't deny success; it directs glory back to God. When you remember your Source, your success will remain secure.

The test of promotion is not how high you climb, but how low you stay before God. Guard your heart, serve others, and let gratitude anchor your greatness.

Action: *Take time today and sincerely thank God for every promotion He has given you. Commit to stay humble.*

Let us pray

1. *Father, thank You for every promotion and opportunity You've given me, in Jesus' name.*
2. *Lord, keep me humble and dependent on You at every level of success, in Jesus' name.*
3. *Father, deliver me from pride, comparison, and self-glory, in Jesus' name.*
4. *Father, let my success reflect Your grace, not my strength, in Jesus' name.*
5. *O Lord, help me to use my promotion to serve others and advance Your Kingdom, in Jesus' name.*

Wednesday 18 March **SOMEONE TO STAND IN THE GAP**

Read: 1 Kings 18:21-24, 36-39

Bible in 1 year: Nah. 1-3
Bible in 2 years: Lev. 1-2

"I looked for someone among them who would build up the wall and stand before me in the gap on behalf of the land so I would not have to destroy it, but I found no one" (Ezekiel 22:30).

God can use one available person to change an entire nation. You may wonder, *"Can someone like me really make a difference?"* History answers clearly: YES. One demonized man, Adolf Hitler, influenced Germany and much of Europe for evil, dragging the world into a war that claimed about 75 million lives. If the devil can use one person to bring destruction, how much more can God use one surrendered life to bring transformation?

God's power through one person is seen clearly in Billy Graham's life. Anointed by God, he became one of the most influential evangelists in history, preaching the gospel across more than 180 countries. Through crusades, radio, and television, billions heard the message of salvation. God used one obedient servant to touch nations and generations.

No nation is beyond God's reach. Israel's history proves this. During the dark days of Ahab and Jezebel, spiritual corruption dominated the land. Yet God raised up one man – Elijah. When fire fell from heaven on Mount Carmel, the people cried, *"The LORD, He is God!"* That moment marked the turning point toward revival and restoration (1 Kings 18).

Just as in Elijah's time, God is still searching today for men and women who will restore broken values and stand in prayer to prevent moral and spiritual collapse. *Building the wall* means strengthening righteousness, truth, and godly leadership where they have been neglected. The real tragedy is not God's judgment, but the shortage of people willing to take responsibility and stand in the gap.

God never said it would take everyone to heal a nation. He said, *"If My people…" (2 Chronicles 7:14).* He did not call first for protests or strategies, but for prayer. When God's people pray, seek His face, and humble themselves, He brings the healing. Our role is simple: pray, believe, and obey.

Action: *Commit to standing in the gap through prayer and righteous living.*

Let us pray

1. *Merciful Father, I worship You because You are the giver of ministries.*
2. *Father, anoint me and use me to impact my generation, in Jesus' name.*
3. *Father, You who used Elijah to bless Israel, use me to bless my nation, in Jesus' name.*
4. *Father, strengthen those You have called to activate the fire of revival in this nation and use them more, in Jesus' name.*
5. *Father, raise righteous men and women like Joseph to help this nation come out of economic captivity.*

Thursday 19 March **3 WEAPONS OF THE ENEMY**

Read: Luke 4:1-13, 28-30

Bible in 1 year: Hab. 1-3
Bible in 2 years: Lev. 3-4

"No weapon formed against you shall prosper, and every tongue which rises against you in judgment you shall condemn. This is the heritage of the servants of the Lord, and their righteousness is from Me, says the Lord" (Isaiah 54:17).

Satan is a defeated foe, yet he still deploys schemes to weaken God's people. Isaiah reminds us that though weapons may be formed, they will not prosper against those who belong to the Lord. Understanding his main strategies equips us to resist the devil with confidence in Christ.

1. ***Seduction:*** The enemy seeks to lure believers into compromise, sin, and false teachings. He tried to seduce Jesus in the wilderness with shortcuts to glory (Luke 4:3-11). Seduction entices the flesh but blinds the spirit. The way to overcome is by submission to God, standing firm in truth, and resisting with the Word.

2. ***Destruction:*** Satan also attempts to eliminate destinies before they bloom. Herod ordered the massacre of innocent children to stop the Messiah (Matthew 2:16). Crowds tried to push Jesus off a cliff (Luke 4:29-30). His goal is premature death or derailment of purpose. But like Jesus, we must pray earnestly and walk under divine

protection. God will frustrate every destructive plan of Satan against you this year.

3. ***Accusation:*** Finally, Satan accuses to paralyze believers psychologically and stirs opposition against them (Revelation 12:10). Jesus was falsely accused of being demon-possessed (John 7:20) and of using Satan's power (Matthew 12:24). Accusations aim to bring shame and silence your voice. The way to conquer is to stand on Christ's righteousness, silence lies with truth, and keep focused on God's assignment.

Many believers testify that once they stopped believing Satan's lies of accusation and instead began to declare God's promises, peace and confidence filled their hearts. The blood of Jesus speaks louder than every false voice.

Every weapon – whether seduction, destruction, or accusation fashioned against you this year will fail, in Jesus' name. Root yourself in God's Word, pray without ceasing, and walk boldly, for the Lord has already secured your victory.

Action: *Set aside at least 30 minutes today to pray with these verses against any satanic attack you are facing right now (Heb. 2:14-15; Rev. 12:11; Deut. 28:7; Rom 8:35-39).*

Let us pray

1. *Father, thank You for the promise that no weapon formed against me will prosper, in Jesus' name.*
2. *Lord, deliver me from every seduction of sin, compromise, and false teaching, in Jesus' name.*
3. *Father, arise, let every destructive demonic plan designed to cut off my destiny prematurely scatter, in Jesus' name.*

4. *I silence every accusing tongue speaking against me and expose the lies of the enemy, in Jesus' name.*
5. *Father, fill me with discernment, strength, and wisdom to overcome every scheme, in Jesus' name.*

Friday 20 March

THE SECRET OF THE HIDDEN LIFE

Read: Colossians 3:1-5

Bible in 1 year: Zeph. 1-3
Bible in 2 years: Lev. 5-6

"For you died, and your life is hidden with Christ in God" (Colossians 3:3).

In the military, stealth technology is used to make aircraft invisible to enemy radar. By using special shapes and coatings, the plane can fly into hostile territory without being detected. As a believer, holiness is your "stealth" coating. When you live a life that is truly consecrated, you are "hidden with Christ." The enemy's radar of temptation and destruction looks for the "heat signature" of the flesh—pride, lust, and anger. When those signals are absent because you have died to self, the enemy finds nothing in you to hook onto.

Holiness is not about being "seen" by men; it is about being "hidden" in God. Jesus lived this hidden life perfectly. He could walk through a crowd that wanted to stone Him because He was perfectly aligned with the Father's will. Many of us struggle with the same recurring battles because we have too much "flesh" exposed. We are too visible to the enemy's radar because we still crave the applause of men or the pleasures of the world. You need to shrink in your own estimation until only Christ is visible.

A life hidden is an invincible life. When you are dead to your own reputation and alive only to God, the "arrows" of criticism, offense, and temptation lose their target. You are no longer easily provoked because there is no "self" left to offend. Today, decide to retreat into the secret place. Let your motives be purified in the hidden chamber of prayer. The more you hide in Christ, the more the power of God will be revealed through you.

Action: *Identify one area where you are currently "seeking attention" or "feeling offended." Intentionally choose to be "hidden" today by doing a kind act in secret or refusing to defend yourself.*

Let us pray

1. *Father, I thank You that my life is safely tucked away in Christ.*
2. *Lord, let every "fleshly signature" in my character be neutralized by Your Spirit.*
3. *Lord, hide me from the eyes of the destroyer and the snares of the fowler.*
4. *Father, help me to die daily to self-will so that Christ may live through me.*
5. *Holy Spirit, draw me deeper into the secret place where my strength is renewed.*

Saturday 21 March

THE ARCHITECTURE OF INTEGRITY

Read: Proverbs 11:1-5;
Amos 7:7-9

Bible in 1 year: Hag. 1-2
Bible in 2 years: Lev. 7-8

"The integrity of the upright will guide them, but the perversity of the unfaithful will destroy them." (Proverbs 11:3)

In construction, a "plumb line" is a simple tool (a weight on a string) used to ensure that a wall is perfectly vertical. A wall can look straight to the naked eye, but if it is even a few millimeters off the vertical axis, the law of gravity will eventually pull the entire structure down as it grows taller. Integrity is the "spiritual plumb line" of holiness. It ensures that your private life aligns perfectly with your public testimony. You cannot build a tall life of "enlargement" if your character is leaning toward compromise.

Many people believe they can "negotiate" with holiness, thinking that a little dishonesty in business or a small exaggeration in a testimony won't hurt. But holiness is not a sliding scale; it is an absolute standard. When you lose your integrity, you lose your spiritual "center of gravity." Without it, you cannot stand the pressure of promotion. God showed the prophet Amos a plumb line in the midst of His people to show that He was measuring their hearts, not just their rituals. True holiness means that if someone were to drop a plumb line through your thoughts, your words, and your actions, they would all fall in a perfectly straight line.

True holiness is "uprightness", meaning vertical alignment with God. Integrity protects you because it removes the "hooks" the enemy uses to drag people down. If there is no lie to cover, there is no fear of exposure. If there is no hidden agenda, there is no room for scandal. Today, let the Holy Spirit check your alignment. Are you the same person in the dark that you are in the light? Build with the plumb line of integrity, and your "house" will stand forever.

Action: *Conduct an "integrity audit" today. Is there a small lie you told recently or a "shortcut" you took? Go back and correct it, regardless of the cost to your pride.*

Let us pray

1. *Father, I thank You that Your Word is the true plumb line for my life.*
2. *Lord, forgive me for every area where I have leaned toward dishonesty or hypocrisy.*
3. *Lord, establish me in integrity and let it be my constant guide.*
4. *Father, remove every crooked way from my heart and make my paths straight.*
5. *Holy Spirit, give me the courage to be truthful even when it is inconvenient.*

Sunday 22 March

THE DISCIPLINE OF THE GATES

Read: Psalm 101:1-4;
Job 31:1-4

Bible in 1 year: Mal. 1-2
Bible in 2 years: Lev. 9-10

"I will set no wicked thing before mine eyes: I hate the work of them that turn aside; it shall not cleave to me." (Psalm 101:3)

In ancient times, a city was only as secure as its gates. Even if the walls were fifty feet thick, an enemy could walk right in if the gatekeepers were asleep or if the gates were left wide open. In the geography of your soul, your eyes and ears are the primary "gates." Holiness is not just a condition of the heart; it is a discipline of the gatekeeper. What you allow to pass through your eyes and ears eventually takes up residence in your heart. If you want a holy heart, you must have holy gates.

Job understood this architecture perfectly. He didn't wait until he was tempted to commit a sin; he made a "covenant with his eyes" beforehand. He set a policy for his gates. Many Christians today wonder why they struggle with lust, envy, or fear, yet they spend hours "feeding" their gates with movies, music, and social media feeds that celebrate those very things. You cannot watch "wicked things" and expect to produce "holy thoughts." To be enlarged in holiness, you must be a ruthless gatekeeper. You must decide that some things are simply not allowed to enter your territory.

Being a gatekeeper means you have the authority to

say "No." When a conversation turns to gossip, you shut the ear-gate. When a screen displays something that triggers the flesh, you shut the eye-gate. This isn't being "old-fashioned"; it is being strategically secure. When your gates are well-guarded, the peace of God can rule undisturbed within your walls. Today, take a look at your "input." Are you guarding your gates, or are they swinging wide for every passing influence? Secure your gates, and you secure your destiny.

Prophetic Declaration: *My eyes shall see only the beauty of holiness! My ears shall hear only the voice of my Shepherd! My gates are closed to the enemy and open to the King of Glory*

Let us pray

1. *Father, I thank You for the wisdom to guard the entrances to my soul.*
2. *Lord, I repent for every "wicked thing" I have intentionally set before my eyes.*
3. *Lord, help me to make a firm covenant with my eyes and my ears today.*
4. *Father, give me the courage to turn away from every unholy influence or conversation.*
5. *Holy Spirit, stand as the chief Watchman over my heart and my gates.*

Monday 23 March **MAYBE YOU NEED REVIVAL**

Read: Revelation 2:1-7

Bible in 1 year: Mal. 3-4
Bible in 2 years: Lev. 11

"I lie in the dust; revive me by your word" (Psalm 119:25)."

Every believer needs revival from time to time to stay on track. Our text reveals that one can fall along the way and lose one's first love. As humans, we are not always consistent in our love for God, His Word, our fervency in the Spirit, and our eagerness to serve Him.

There is an urgent need to seek God for the revival of your soul when your fire begins to die. You may have noticed that you no longer pray with fervency or that you fall asleep during prayer, even after a good rest.

When you notice that sin is becoming attractive to you – you are easily enticed by the sinful practices you had earlier forsaken because of your commitment to follow Jesus Christ, it is a sign that you need revival. Maybe you struggle to give a tithe of your income to God or to support His work, despite the blessings He lavishes on you daily.

When you are no longer eager to go to the house of God like David, who said, *"I was glad when they said to me, 'Let us go into the house of the LORD" (Psalm 122:1).* When you are absent from fellowship, and your heart is not disturbed, it is a sign that you need revival.

When you notice that your love for other believers has become cold or you find resentment, unforgiveness, or bitterness cropping up in your heart, it is time to pray for revival.

When you are no longer eager to witness and win the lost for Jesus Christ, or you drag your feet when your church announces an evangelistic outreach, then it is time to seek revival.

The Lord Jesus Christ is saying to you today, *"Remember therefore from where you have fallen; repent and do the first works" (Revelation 2:5).* He will forgive you and baptize you with new fire.

Action: *Take time and examine your life, then repent concerning any issue the Holy Spirit points out to you.*

Let us pray

1. *My Father and LORD of my life, I worship You because You can keep my soul from destruction.*
2. *O Lord my God, I need a spiritual revival; touch my soul with Your fire and revive me today, in the name of Jesus.*
3. *Dear Holy Spirit, illuminate the eyes of my heart and help me to see where I have fallen, in the name of Jesus.*
4. *Place your hand on your heart and pray, "Father, set me on fire again for worship, service, and evangelism, in the name of Jesus."*
5. *Raise your hand and pray 5 times, "I receive fresh fire now to become an agent of revival in my church and community, in the name of Jesus."*

Prophetic Prayers of the Week

1. **"Sanctify them by Your truth." (John 17:17).** *I am rooted and established in God's truth, in Jesus' name.*

2. **"The entrance of Your words gives light." (Psalm 119:130).** *I am walking in God's light and revelation; darkness will not rule me, in Jesus' name.*
3. **"God gives wisdom to all who ask." (James 1:5).** *I operate in divine wisdom, in Jesus' name.*

Tuesday 24 March

THE FELLOWSHIP OF LIGHT

Read: 1 John 1:5-7;
2 Corinthians 6:14-18

Bible in 1 year: Job. 28-31
Bible in 2 years: Lev. 12-13

"But if we walk in the light as He is in the light, we have fellowship with one another, and the blood of Jesus Christ His Son cleanses us from all sin." (1 John 1:7)

If you take a piece of white chalk and rub it against a piece of charcoal, the chalk doesn't make the charcoal white; instead, the charcoal makes the chalk black. This is a simple law of contamination. In our spiritual walk, holiness is heavily influenced by our "fellowship." You cannot expect to burn with a holy fire if you are constantly surrounding yourself with "wet blankets"—people who dampen your passion for God, mock your consecration, or lure you back into the shadows of compromise. To be enlarged in holiness, you must be intentional about the "light" you walk in and the people you walk with.

Walking in the light means living a life of transparency. It is the refusal to have a "hidden" side that you are ashamed of. Darkness is the breeding ground for sin; it is where mold grows and where secrets fester. But the moment you bring a struggle into the light—through confession and accountability—the power of that sin is broken. Many people remain stuck in cycles of defeat because they are trying to be "holy" in isolation. True enlargement happens in the context of holy fellowship, where we sharpen one another and keep each other in the light of God's Word.

Choosing holy associations is not about being "holier-than-thou"; it is about spiritual survival. If your closest friends are comfortable with sin, you will eventually become comfortable with it too. But if you walk with those who are "in the light," you will find that the blood of Jesus is constantly at work, cleansing your conscience and keeping your path bright. Today, evaluate your inner circle. Are they helping you stay in the light, or are they dragging you into the shadows? Surround yourself with the light, and you will become a beacon of holiness to the world.

Action: *Identify one relationship that consistently drains your spiritual strength or encourages compromise, set a polite boundary today, and use that time to fellowship with a believer who inspires you toward holiness.*

Let us pray

1. *Father, I thank You that You are Light and in You there is no darkness at all.*
2. *Lord, deliver me from every unholy alliance that is dimming my spiritual light.*
3. *Lord, bring God-fearing people into my life who will sharpen my walk with You.*
4. *Father, give me the grace to live a transparent life, free from the power of secrets.*
5. *Holy Spirit, let the blood of Jesus cleanse me continually as I walk in the light today.*

Wednesday 25 March **THE POWER OF "NO"**

Read: Titus 2:11-14

Bible in 1 year: Job. 32-34
Bible in 2 years: Lev. 14

"Teaching us that, denying ungodliness and worldly lusts, we should live soberly, righteously, and godly in the present age" (Titus 2:12)

In the world of art, a masterpiece is created not just by what the sculptor adds, but by what he chips away. To reach the beautiful statue hidden within the marble block, the artist must say "no" to excess stone. Holiness works the same way. The grace of God is not just a "buffer" for our sins; it is a teacher that instructs us to say "no." To walk in holiness, your "no" must be as strong as your "yes." You cannot say "yes" to God's best until you have the courage to say "no" to the world's "good enough."

Many believers struggle because they have a "leaky No." They say no to temptation on Sunday, but by Tuesday, that "no" has faded into a "maybe." Joseph in Egypt had a "solid No." When Potiphar's wife pressured him day after day, his refusal wasn't based on fear of being caught, but on his loyalty to God. He said, "How then can I do this great wickedness, and sin against God?" His "no" to a moment of pleasure was his "yes" to a lifetime of palace authority. Every time you deny a worldly lust, you are not losing out; you are clearing the marble to reveal the masterpiece of Christ in you.

Holiness is the "sober" life. It means you are clear-headed and not "drunk" on the values of this world. When the world says, "everyone is doing it," the holy person is sober enough to see the trap. Your ability to say "no" to ungodliness is the evidence that grace is truly working in you. Today, don't look at holiness as a list of "don'ts," but as a series of strategic "no's" that protect your "yes" to God. The more you deny the flesh, the more room you make for the Spirit to expand your territory.

Prophetic Declaration: *My "No" is final! My "Yes" to God is absolute! I walk in victory over every worldly lust!*

Let us pray

1. *Father, I thank You for the grace that teaches me to live righteously.*
2. *Lord, strengthen my "No" against every subtle temptation today.*
3. *Lord, deliver me from the craving for worldly approval and lusts.*
4. *Father, help me to live soberly and keep my spiritual focus sharp.*
5. *Holy Spirit, empower me to chip away everything that hides Your glory in me.*

Thursday 26 March

KINGDOM VALUES IN A CORRUPT SYSTEM

Read: Romans 12:1-2

Bible in 1 year: Job 35-37
Bible in 2 years: Lev. 15-16

"But Daniel resolved that he would not defile himself with the king's food, or with the wine that he drank. Therefore he asked the chief of the eunuchs to allow him not to defile himself" (Daniel 1:8).

Every believer in the marketplace faces pressure to conform. In a world driven by greed, manipulation, and deceit, standing for truth can seem costly. Yet, this is where true Kingdom greatness is tested. God calls His children to shine by living according to His values, not the world's corrupt systems. To succeed in a dirty world without getting stained is the believer's true victory.

Daniel lived in Babylon, a pagan empire marked by idolatry and compromise, yet *"he purposed in his heart not to defile himself" (Daniel 1:8).* His decision to honor God gave him divine promotion. When you choose righteousness in a corrupt environment, you may lose temporary favor with men, but you gain eternal favor with God. Kingdom values – truth, justice, humility, and compassion are not negotiable; they are our identity.

A Christian civil servant shared how he was constantly pressured to falsify documents for profit. Each time, he refused politely, saying, "My integrity is my inheritance." Years later, when a new administration sought honest officers for key positions, he was promoted. His integrity spoke louder than his résumé. That's how the Kingdom advances – through character, not compromise.

Corruption may look rewarding, but it destroys destiny. God is raising Daniels in this generation. Men and women who will stand clean in dirty systems, who will lead by righteousness and lift their nations by example. When you live by Kingdom values, you become a standard others measure by.

Child of God, do not blend in to survive; stand out to make a difference. The God who promotes the pure in heart will defend your name and enlarge your influence.

Action: *Is there a standard God wants you to establish in your work? Decide to do it today.*

Let us pray

1. *Father, thank You for making me a light in dark systems, in Jesus' name.*
2. *Father, strengthen me to stand for truth even when it costs me, in Jesus' name.*
3. *O Lord, let Kingdom values rule my heart, speech, and work.*
4. *Father, deliver me from every temptation to compromise, in Jesus' name.*
5. *I decree that I will uphold Kingdom standards and prosper by divine integrity, in Jesus' name.*

Friday 27 March

THE WEIGHT OF THE CROWN

Read: Leviticus 21:10-12;
2 Timothy 2:3-4

Bible in 1 year: Job 38-42
Bible in 2 years: Lev. 17-18

"Neither shall he go out of the sanctuary, nor profane the sanctuary of his God; for the crown of the anointing oil of his God is upon him" (Leviticus 21:12).

In the Old Testament, the High Priest was under stricter rules than the average person. He couldn't participate in certain mourning rituals or let his hair hang loose. This wasn't because God loved him more, but because he carried the "crown of the anointing oil." The higher the office, the greater the restriction. Holiness is the "weight" of the crown you carry. You cannot expect to carry a heavyweight anointing while living a lightweight lifestyle. To be enlarged in authority, you must accept the "holy constraints" that come with being a carrier of God's Presence.

Many people want the "oil" (the power), but they reject the "crown" (the responsibility of holiness). They want to do what everyone else does—watch what they watch, talk how they talk, and go where they go—and still expect the demons to tremble when they speak. But the spirit realm recognizes the "crown." Demons didn't just fear Jesus because He was the Son of God; they feared Him because there was no "profanity" in His sanctuary. He was perfectly consecrated. When you accept the restrictions of holiness, you aren't being imprisoned; you are being enthroned.

Consecration means you are no longer your own. You are a "sanctuary." Just as a King's palace is not a public park, your life is not a place where every worldly thought or habit is allowed to loiter. Some things that are "permissible" for others are "unlawful" for you because of the oil on your head. This month, stop complaining about the things you "can't do" and start celebrating the "crown" you carry. The more you honor the sanctuary of your heart, the more God will honor the words of your mouth.

Action: *Identify one common habit you've kept because "everyone does it," and surrender it today as an act of royal consecration.*

Let us pray

1. *Father, I thank You for the crown of anointing You have placed upon my life.*
2. *Lord, help me to respect the holy restrictions that come with Your Presence.*
3. *Lord, deliver me from the desire to be "like everyone else" at the expense of my oil.*
4. *Father, let the sanctuary of my heart be holy and unprofaned by worldly habits.*
5. *Holy Spirit, remind me of my royal identity whenever I am tempted to compromise.*

Saturday 28 March **THE BEAUTY OF BATTLEMENTS**

Read: Deuteronomy 22:8;
1 Corinthians 8:9-13

Bible in 1 year: Mark 1-3
Bible in 2 years: Lev. 19-20

"When you build a new house, then you shall make a battlement for your roof, that you may not bring guilt of bloodshed on your house if anyone falls from it." (Deuteronomy 22:8)

In biblical times, the roof of a house was a place of fellowship and rest. God commanded that a "battlement" (a low wall or railing) be built around the edge. This wasn't because the roof was bad, but because the edge was dangerous. Holiness is the "battlement" of your life. It is the safety rail that prevents you and those following you from falling into disaster. Do you care enough about your soul and your neighbor's safety to build boundaries around your freedom?

Many people argue for their "rights" to engage in certain behaviors, saying, "The Bible doesn't explicitly forbid this!" But holiness asks a higher question: "Is this safe for my soul and the souls of those watching me?" A person of integrity doesn't see how close they can get to the edge without falling; they build a wall far back from the ledge. Your "battlement" might be a decision never to be alone with someone of the opposite sex, or a filter on your internet. These aren't signs of weakness; they are signs of architectural wisdom.

If you don't build battlements, you bring

"bloodguilt" to your house. This means your lack of boundaries can cause a younger believer to stumble or your own family to suffer the consequences of your fall. Holiness is the ultimate act of love for your household. By setting high standards for your conduct, you create a "safe roof" where the presence of God can dwell without the threat of a sudden tragedy. Today, check your "roof." Have you left any edges unguarded? Build a battlement today and secure your future.

Action: *Identify one "legal" but "dangerous" area of your life and put a firm boundary (a battlement) around it today.*

Let us pray

1. *Father, I thank You for the laws that protect me from falling.*
2. *Lord, give me the wisdom to build "battlements" around my freedom.*
3. *Lord, help me to live in a way that never causes a brother to stumble.*
4. *Father, let my household be safe from the "bloodguilt" of compromise.*
5. *Holy Spirit, show me the "edges" in my life that need a stronger boundary.*

Sunday 29 March

THE HOLINESS OF THE HARVEST

Read: Leviticus 19:9-10;
John 15:1-5

Bible in 1 year: Mark 4-6
Bible in 2 years: Lev. 21-22

"And when you reap the harvest of your land, you shall not wholly reap the corners of your field... you shall leave them for the poor and stranger: I am the Lord your God." (Leviticus 19:9-10)

In God's economy, holiness is tied to how we handle our "corners." In the Old Testament, a holy farmer was one who left the edges of his field unharvested so the needy could eat. Holiness was not just about what the farmer didn't do (sin); it was about what he did with his abundance. God wants you to move from a "mine-centered" life to a "God-centered" life. True purity is seen in the generosity of our spirit. If you are stingy, greedy, or selfish, your "field" might be productive, but your heart is not yet holy.

A holy life is a "fruitful" life. Jesus said that the branch that abides in Him—the Holy Vine—will bring forth much fruit. But fruit is never for the tree itself; it is for others to consume. If you claim to be growing in holiness, there must be a visible "harvest" of kindness, patience, and resources that others can benefit from. When we refuse to help the "stranger" or the "poor" because we are too focused on our own accumulation, we are profaning the harvest God gave us. Holiness means acknowledging that everything we have is a trust from "the Lord your God."

When you leave your "corners" for God's purposes,

you aren't losing profit; you are gaining a partner. God becomes the Guarantor of your field when you honor His heart for the broken. Your enlargement is not just for your comfort; it is to increase your capacity to be a blessing.

Today, ask yourself: Am I reaping my field "wholly" for myself, or am I leaving room for God's mercy to flow through me? A holy heart is a generous heart.

Action: *Identify a "corner" of your time or finances today and give it to someone in need without expecting anything back.*

Let us pray

1. *Father, I thank You for being the Source of every harvest in my life.*
2. *Lord, deliver me from the spirit of greed and "me-centered" living.*
3. *Lord, enlarge my heart to be generous to the poor and the stranger.*
4. *Father, help me to see my resources as a tool for Your holy purposes.*
5. *Holy Spirit, make me a fruitful branch that brings glory to the Vine.*

Monday 30 March **SHOW COMPASSION TO OTHERS**

Read: Matthew 14:14-16

Bible in 1 year: Mark 7-10
Bible in 2 years: Lev. 23

"The generous will prosper; those who refresh others will themselves be refreshed." (Proverbs 11:25, NLT).

Compassion is love in action. It is the ability to see beyond people's faults and respond to their needs with mercy and kindness. Compassion is key to expansion.

Matthew 14:14 says, *"And Jesus went forth, and saw a great multitude, and was moved with compassion toward them, and he healed their sick."* Compassion did not allow Him to look away; it compelled Him to act – He healed their sick.

A believer who walks in compassion becomes a channel through which God touches lives. Your love for God secures your place with Him, but your compassion for people determines your impact on earth. Selfishness shrinks influence; compassion enlarges it. Scripture teaches that those who refresh others will be refreshed themselves. God builds reservoirs for those who choose to become rivers.

Jesus' ministry was fueled by compassion. He healed the sick, fed the hungry, touched the rejected, and defended the broken. Compassion made Him stop for blind Bartimaeus, weep at Lazarus' tomb, and forgive those who crucified Him. To follow Christ is to carry His heart for people.

Many Christians lose spiritual power and relevance because they grow insensitive to human suffering. Yet

Mother Teresa rightly observed, "The greatest poverty is to feel unwanted and unloved." Compassion heals this poverty. When you become a channel of blessing for the poor, God ensures that you never lack help.

Proverbs 11:25 is a spiritual law: generosity attracts divine supply. Compassion is never wasted; it returns multiplied. When you open your heart to others, God opens the heavens over you. The hand that gives water will never run dry.

Beloved, ask God to soften your heart again. Let your home, your words, and your actions reflect God's mercy. Compassion is not weakness; it is the strength of Christ expressed through love.

Action: *Spend time today asking God to soften your heart and make you more compassionate toward others.*

Let us pray

1. *Father, thank You for Your mercy and compassion toward me, in Jesus' name.*
2. *Fill my heart and my family with genuine compassion, in Jesus' name.*
3. *Lord deliver me from selfishness and hardness of heart, in Jesus' name.*
4. *Father, use me as an instrument of comfort and help to the hurting, in Jesus' name.*
5. *Father, let my home become a refuge of love and mercy, in Jesus' name.*

Prophetic Prayers of the Week

1. ***"The LORD is my light and my salvation." (Psalm 27:1).*** *Nothing will cause me to fear or flee, in Jesus' name.*

2. ***"He gives His angels charge over you." (Psalm 91:11).*** *My family and I are escorted today by God's angels, in Jesus' name.*
3. ***"Christ has redeemed us from the curse." (Galatians 3:13).*** *No curse will stand in my life, in Jesus' name.*

Tuesday 31 March

THE DISCIPLINE OF THE TONGUE

Read: James 3:1-12;
Psalm 141:3-4

Bible in 1 year: Mark 11-13
Bible in 2 years: (Catch-up)

"Set a guard, O Lord, over my mouth; keep watch over the door of my lips" (Psalm 141:3)

A small rudder controls a massive ship, and a tiny spark can set an entire forest ablaze. In the same way, the tongue is the "steering wheel" of your holiness. You cannot claim to have a consecrated heart while having a "loose" tongue. Holiness is not just about where your feet go or what your eyes see; it is about what your mouth releases. If you spend your day speaking words of bitterness, gossip, or "dirty" jokes, you are essentially pouring ink into a glass of pure water. To be enlarged in holiness, you must surrender your vocabulary to the Holy Spirit.

Many believers struggle to see the power of God in their lives because they "nullify" their prayers with their conversations. They pray for "enlargement" in the morning but speak "limitations" and "complaints" in the afternoon. A holy tongue is a "healed" tongue. It is one that refuses to participate in the assassination of another person's character. It is a tongue that speaks truth even when a lie would be more convenient. When you "set a guard" over your mouth, you are acknowledging that your words are seeds that will eventually produce a harvest in your environment.

If you want to walk in a higher level of authority,

start by disciplining your speech. Before you speak, ask: "Is it true? Is it kind? Is it necessary? Is it holy?" When you keep the "door of your lips" closed to ungodliness, you create a vacuum that the Holy Spirit fills with prophetic insight and grace. A person who can control their tongue is a "perfect man," able to bridle the whole body. Today, let your speech be "seasoned with salt," bringing flavor and healing to everyone you encounter.

Action: *Go through the entire day today without speaking a single negative word about anyone, including yourself.*

Let us pray

1. *Father, I thank You for the power of life and death that resides in my tongue.*
2. *Lord, I repent for every idle and unholy word I have spoken in the past.*
3. *Lord, set a supernatural guard over my mouth and the door of my lips.*
4. *Father, let the words of my mouth and the meditation of my heart be acceptable to You.*
5. *Holy Spirit, help me to speak words that build up and never tear down.*

Wednesday 1 April **THE BLOOD THAT SPEAKS**

Read: Exodus 12:12-13

Bible in 1 year: Isa. 16-18
Bible in 2 years: Lev. 24; 25:1-28

"To Jesus the Mediator of the new covenant, and to the blood of sprinkling that speaks better things than that of Abel" (Hebrews 12:24).

The Blood of Jesus is not silent; it speaks. From the altar of heaven, it continually declares mercy, forgiveness, and victory for those who belong to Christ. While the blood of Abel cried out for vengeance, the Blood of Jesus cries out for redemption. It silences every accusation of the enemy and announces that the debt of sin you owed has been paid in full.

In the Old Testament, the blood of lambs offered a temporary covering, but in Christ, we have a permanent cleansing. His Blood establishes a covenant that cannot be broken. Every time the believer pleads the Blood, he is invoking divine testimony in his favor. The Blood speaks in the courts of heaven, in the battles of life, and in the depths of conscience. It covers, cleanses, and conquers.

When the Israelites marked their doors with the lamb's blood, death could not enter. That same power operates today. The Blood of Jesus breaks curses, cancels evil verdicts, and restores peace. It is your weapon of defense and your seal of eternal life. You overcome the accuser *"by the blood of the Lamb and by the word of your testimony" (Revelation 12:11).*

Did someone tell you that you are struggling in life because there are evil altars speaking against you? The truth is that what the blood of Jesus is speaking for the believer is more powerful than what evil altars are saying. Beloved, believe what the blood is saying and not what the enemy is saying.

Action: *Spend time today declaring the blood of Jesus over the various areas of your life and family.*

Let us pray

1. *Thank You, Jesus, for the speaking power of Your Blood.*
2. *Father, let the Blood of Jesus silence every voice of accusation against me.*
3. *Father, cover my home, family, and destiny with Your redeeming Blood.*
4. *By the Blood, I overcome fear, guilt, and condemnation, in Jesus' name.*
5. *Father, arise in my family, let every evil covenant be broken by the superior covenant of Your Blood.*

Thursday 2 April **THE HIGH COST OF SIN**

Read: 2 Samuel 12:9-15

Bible in 1 year: Isa. 19-21
Bible in 2 years: Lev. 25:29-55; 26:1-22

"For the wages of sin is death, but the gift of God is eternal life in Christ Jesus our Lord" (Romans 6:23 NIV).

Sin promises pleasure but pays in pain. David's sin with Bathsheba was forgiven, but the consequences echoed for years. His family was torn apart by violence, betrayal, and grief. Forgiveness cancels guilt, but it does not always erase consequences. This is the high cost of sin.

The Hebrew word for "wages", '*Sakhar*', refers to "payment, hire, or reward." Sin is a cruel master that pays its servants in sorrow, shame, and death. Like a poisoned meal, it may taste sweet at first, but it kills slowly.

David wept bitterly when his infant son died. Later, his household was ravaged by incest, murder, and rebellion. One act of disobedience opened a floodgate of suffering. The enemy hides the price tag of sin, showing only the short-lived pleasure, not the long-term ruin.

A man once stole a loaf of bread to satisfy hunger, but ended up in prison for years. His temporary relief became a lifelong tragedy. So, it is with sin. It costs more than we are willing to pay and keeps us longer than we want to stay.

Yet, Christ paid the ultimate cost for us on the cross. His blood offers us freedom from sin's wages and power.

We must walk in His grace, soberly counting the cost, and choosing holiness.

Action: *Is there a sin Satan has lured you into? Decide today to put an end to it. Seek help if you are trapped.*

Let us pray

1. *Father, thank You for giving me victory over sin and the devil through the blood of Jesus Christ.*
2. *O Lord, help me to see sin as You see it, in Jesus' name.*
3. *Father, please deliver me from hidden snares that lead to destruction, in Jesus' name.*
4. *Father, arise and let the blood of Jesus Christ wipe out every ripple effect of disobedience from my family, in Jesus' name.*
5. *I reclaim the restoration of every virtue and blessing stolen by Satan from my family, in Jesus' name.*

Friday 3 April

THE PRICE OF OUR REDEMPTION

Read: Isaiah 53:3-6

Bible in 1 year: Isa. 22-24
Bible in 2 years: Lev. 26:23-46; 27

"But He was wounded for our transgressions, He was bruised for our iniquities; the chastisement for our peace was upon Him, and by His stripes we are healed." (Isaiah 53:5).

Easter begins, not at the empty tomb, but at the cross. Before there was resurrection power, there was sacrificial suffering. The cross reveals the true cost of our redemption. Our sins were not ignored; they were judged by God. Humanity was not abandoned; we were rescued at the price of Jesus' blood.

Isaiah prophesied centuries before Jesus Christ that the Messiah would suffer for us. Jesus Christ hung on the cross bearing unbearable pain, rejection, and the crushing weight of the sins of the whole world, choosing obedient love over escape so humanity could be redeemed. In that sacred moment of agony and silence, the Innocent suffered for the guilty, fulfilling the words: ***"He was pierced for our transgressions, He was crushed for our iniquities; the punishment that brought us peace was on Him" (Isaiah 53:5).*** Jesus did not die for His own sins; He had none. He died as our substitute. Every wound inflicted on Him addressed our transgressions. Every bruise paid for our iniquities. The punishment that should have fallen on us was placed on Him so that we could have peace with God.

The Hebrew idea behind "Wounded" carries the sense of being pierced through. Christ was pierced not only by nails and a spear, but by the weight of our guilt. The cross, therefore, is not merely a symbol of suffering; it is the altar of divine love. At Calvary, justice and mercy met. God remained righteous while saving sinners.

Many people celebrate Easter without stopping at the cross. Yet without the cross, the resurrection has no meaning. Forgiveness, healing, reconciliation, and restoration all flow from the blood Jesus shed. Grace is free to us, but it was costly to Him.

When we look at the cross, pride dies, gratitude rises, and worship becomes sincere. The cross reminds us that we are deeply loved and fully redeemed.

Action: *Jesus died for the salvation of the whole world. Share the good news with at least one person today.*

Let us pray

1. *Father, thank You for loving me enough to give Your Son for my redemption.*
2. *Lord Jesus, I receive afresh the forgiveness purchased by Your blood.*
3. *Father, let the power of the cross destroy every guilt and condemnation in my life, in Jesus' name.*
4. *O Lord, heal every broken area of my life through the finished work of Calvary, in Jesus' name.*
5. *Father, help me live a life worthy of the price You paid for me, in Jesus' name.*

Saturday 4 April **IT IS FINISHED!**

Read: John 19:28-30

Bible in 1 year: Isa. 25-27
Bible in 2 years: Mark 1

"So, when Jesus had received the sour wine, He said, 'It is finished!' And bowing His head, He gave up His spirit" (John 19:30).

When Jesus cried out, *"It is finished,"* He was not sighing in exhaustion; He was declaring victory. The Greek word used is *'Tetelestai,'* a powerful term meaning "Paid in full, completed, fully accomplished." In the marketplace, it was written across a bill when a debt was fully settled. On the cross, Jesus stamped *'Tetelestai'* over humanity's greatest debt – sin.

At that moment, the work of redemption was completed. The demands of the law were satisfied. The penalty for sin was fully paid. Satan's legal hold over humanity was broken. Salvation was not postponed or partial; it was perfected. Nothing needed to be added. Nothing could be improved. The cross was enough.

Many believers still live as though something is unfinished – struggling under guilt, trying to earn God's approval, or punishing themselves for past failures. Easter reminds us that forgiveness is complete, grace is sufficient, and reconciliation with God is secured. We do not fight for victory; we live from victory.

Because the work is finished, we can rest. Because the price is paid, we are free. Because Christ completed the work, we can walk in confidence, gratitude, and obedience; not to be saved, but because we are saved.

The empty tomb confirms what the cross declared: the work is done.

Action: *Stop trying to earn what Christ has already completed and rest in His finished work today.*

Let us pray

1. *Father, thank You for the finished work of Christ on the cross.*
2. *Lord Jesus, I receive the fullness of Your forgiveness and grace.*
3. *I renounce guilt, condemnation, and self-effort, in Jesus' name.*
4. *Dear Holy Spirit, help me live daily from the victory of the cross, in Jesus' name.*
5. *Jesus has paid the full price for my freedom; I break free from every satanic manipulation, in Jesus' name.*

Sunday 5 April **THE POWER OF RESURRECTION**

Read: Luke 22:54-62

Bible in 1 year: Isa. 28-30
Bible in 2 years: Mark 2-3

"That I may know Him and the power of His resurrection, and the fellowship of His sufferings, being conformed to His death" (Philippians 3:10).

Easter is not only a historical event to be remembered; it is a spiritual power to be experienced. The resurrection of Jesus Christ released divine power that conquered sin, defeated death, and shattered the authority of the grave. This same resurrection power is now at work in every believer through the Holy Spirit. *"How very great is his power at work in us who believe. This power working in us is the same as the mighty strength which he used when he raised Christ from death and seated him at his right side in the heavenly world" (Ephesians 1:19-20 GNT).*

The power of the resurrection is the power of new life. It transforms hearts, breaks old patterns, and enables believers to live above sin and fear. Christianity is not merely a moral improvement of the old life; it is the impartation of a new life. As Paul desired, knowing Christ includes experiencing the power that raised Him from the dead.

Before the resurrection, Peter was fearful and unstable. He denied Jesus three times under pressure and threats (Luke 22:54-62). Yet after the resurrection and the outpouring of the Holy Spirit, Peter was radically transformed. In Acts 2, the same man who once feared a servant girl stood boldly before thousands, proclaiming

Christ without fear. What changed? It was resurrection power at work in him. The resurrection turned a coward into a courageous witness and a failure into a leader.

The resurrection power of Christ does not remove challenges, but it gives strength to overcome them. It empowers us to forgive, endure suffering, live holy lives, and fulfill our God-given assignments. Easter assures us that no situation is too dead for God to revive.

Action: *Today, take some time to pray insistently about a dead situation in your life. God will resurrect it!*

Let us pray

1. *Father, thank You for the power released to me through the resurrection of Jesus Christ.*
2. *Lord, let resurrection power bring life to every dead area of my life, in Jesus' name.*
3. *Dear Holy Spirit, empower me to live victoriously over sin and fear, in Jesus' name.*
4. *Father, as You transformed Peter, transform me into an effective witness for Christ, in Jesus' name.*
5. *I declare that the power that raised Christ from the dead is working in me, in Jesus' name.*

Monday 6 April **RISEN TO LIVE FOR GOD**

Read: Romans 6:1-11

Bible in 1 year: Isa. 31-33
Bible in 2 years: Mark 4

"Just as Christ was raised from the dead by the glory of the Father, even so we also should walk in newness of life" (Romans 6:4).

The resurrection of Jesus Christ was not only about Him rising from the grave; it was about us rising with Him into a new way of life. Easter calls believers to transformation, not just celebration. Salvation is not an excuse to continue in sin; it is an invitation to live differently. Paul makes it clear that those who are united with Christ in His death are also united with Him in His resurrection (Romans 6:5). This means our old life, dominated by sin, selfishness, and disobedience, was crucified with Christ, and a new life empowered by grace has begun. Resurrection life is visible in our choices, attitudes, and conduct.

When Zacchaeus encountered Jesus, his life changed immediately (Luke 19:1-9). Though his meeting occurred before the crucifixion, it illustrates resurrection life in action. He repented publicly, restored what he had stolen, and committed to righteous living. Jesus declared, *"Today salvation has come to this house" (Luke 19:9).* New life produces new behavior.

Once bound by darkness, Mary Magdalene became one of the first witnesses of the risen Christ **(John 20:11-18)**. Her encounter with the resurrected Jesus transformed her sorrow into purpose. She went from mourning at the tomb to proclaiming, *"I have seen the Lord" (John 20:18)*. Resurrection life turns broken people into messengers of hope.

After the resurrection, believers lived differently. They walked in unity, generosity, and bold witness. Scripture says, *"With great power the apostles gave witness to the resurrection of the Lord Jesus" (Acts 4:33)*. A resurrected Christ produced a resurrected lifestyle.

Easter challenges us to ask: Are we living the old life, or walking in newness of life?

Action: *Identify an old habit and put it away. Begin to practice one new Christlike behavior as evidence of the resurrection life in you.*

Let us pray

1. *Father, thank You that I am raised with Christ into newness of life.*
2. *Father, by the power of the resurrection, break every old, sinful pattern in me, in Jesus' name.*
3. *Holy Spirit, help me live daily in obedience and holiness, in Jesus' name.*
4. *I choose to live for God, not for sin, in Jesus' name.*
5. *I rise above satanic limitations and the works of the flesh by the power of resurrection at work in me, in Jesus' name.*

Prophetic Prayers of the Week

1. ***"The path of the just shines brighter." (Proverbs 4:18).*** *My destiny is shining brighter and clearer, in Jesus' name.*
2. ***"The LORD bless you and keep you." (Numbers 6:24).*** *I am blessed by God; no man or woman can curse me, in Jesus' name.*
3. ***"Greater is He who is in you." (1 John 4:4).*** *Nothing will intimidate me today, in Jesus' name.*

Tuesday 7 April

LOVE: THE FOUNDATION FOR A BLESSED FAMILY

Read: 1 Corinthians 13:4-8

Bible in 1 year: Isa. 34-36
Bible in 2 years: Mark 5

"And now abide faith, hope, love, these three; but the greatest of these is love." *(1 Corinthians 13:13).*

Every truly blessed family rests on one unshakable foundation: **love**. Not money. Not education. Not titles. Scripture is clear; l*ove is the greatest.* When love is absent, even the most prayerful home becomes fragile. Where love reigns, even imperfect families thrive. Do you want your family to prosper? Do everything you can to cultivate genuine, practical love.

The Bible describes love as patient, kind, selfless, forgiving, and enduring (1 Corinthians 13:4–8). This is not natural human affection; it is agape – the God-kind of love. *'Agape'* means unconditional, sacrificial, and deliberate love. It is not based on feelings but on a choice empowered by God. Romans 5:5 tells us that this love is poured into our hearts by the Holy Spirit.

Many family conflicts are not caused by the devil. They are a result of the absence of divine love. Harsh words, unforgiveness, pride, jealousy, and competition slowly choke God's blessing in the family. Love, however, absorbs offenses and keeps relationships alive. That is why Romans 8:28 promises that *all things work together for good*, not for everyone, but for those who love God.

Joseph's story in Genesis 45:4-8, illustrates this truth. Betrayed by his brothers and separated from his family, Joseph chose love instead of bitterness. Years later, that love restored the very family that wounded him. Woah! Love healed what envy and hatred destroyed.

Your family will become resilient if you build it on sincere love. Love will create an atmosphere where children feel safe, spouses feel honored, and God reigns among you. Love does not deny faults, but it refuses to magnify them. Love builds bridges where anger builds walls.

Beloved, do everything to restore love in your family, and blessings will flow again. God does not bless homes filled with strife. He delights in families that walk in love. When love becomes your lifestyle, heaven partners with your household.

Action: *Choose one practical way today to demonstrate love in your family.*

Let us pray

1. *Father, thank You for loving my family unconditionally, in Jesus' name.*
2. *Lord, heal every wound and division in my home by Your love, in Jesus' name.*
3. *Fill our hearts with agape love through the Holy Spirit, in Jesus' name.*
4. *O Lord, remove bitterness, pride, and strife from our family, in Jesus' name.*
5. *Father, teach us to love one another as Christ loves us, in Jesus' name.*

Wednesday 8 April

7 THINGS YOU SHOULD NOT SAY TO YOUR SPOUSE

Read: Ephesians 4:29-32

Bible in 1 year: Isa. 37-39
Bible in 2 years: Mark 6

"Let your conversation be always full of grace, seasoned with salt, so that you may know how to answer everyone" (Colossians 4:6 NIV).

Words are seeds in marriage. What spouses repeatedly say to each other either nourishes love or poisons intimacy. Scripture warns us to avoid corrupt speech and to speak what builds up (Ephesians 4:29). Many marriages are wounded not by major crises but by small, repeated phrases spoken in anger, sarcasm, or contempt.

Here are seven damaging things you should not say to your spouse:

1. "You are just like your father/mother" (said negatively). This transfers resentment and shames your spouse by blaming them for someone else's faults.
2. "You never do anything right." Absolute statements condemn the person rather than correcting behavior.
3. "I regret marrying you." These words strike at the covenant itself, creating deep insecurity.
4. "You are useless/irresponsible." Labels attack dignity and erode mutual respect.
5. "I don't care." This communicates emotional withdrawal and indifference.

6. "If not for me, you would be nothing." Pride and control replace partnership and honor.
7. "God will judge you" (used as a weapon).

Spiritualizing criticism distorts God's character and hardens hearts. Marriage thrives on grace-filled communication. God does not relate to us with contempt; He corrects with patience and truth. When spouses speak harshly, trust erodes, and walls go up. But the same mouth that wounds can also heal. Apology, repentance, and intentional words of affirmation invite the Holy Spirit to restore what was damaged.

Healing begins when we choose humility over pride and love over the urge to win an argument. As you submit your tongues to God, your home will be renewed, and your marriage will grow stronger.

Action: *Apologize sincerely for any hurtful words you have spoken and intentionally affirm one strength of your spouse every day this week.*

Let us pray

1. *Father, thank You for the gift of marriage and Your grace that restores, in Jesus' name.*
2. *Lord, forgive me for every harmful word I have spoken to my spouse, in Jesus' name.*
3. *Father, heal every wound caused by negative speech and restore trust and tenderness, in Jesus' name.*
4. *Father, grant us self-control and wisdom to speak words that build and unite, in Jesus' name.*
5. *O Lord, let our marriage be filled with grace, honor, and peace, in Jesus' name.*

Thursday 9 April

DON'T SAY THESE THINGS TO YOUR CHILD

Read: Proverbs 18:21

Bible in 1 year: Rom. 1-4
Bible in 2 years: Mark 7-8

"Do not let any unwholesome talk come out of your mouths, but only what is helpful for building others up according to their needs" (Ephesians 4:29 NIV).

Words are seeds. Every sentence spoken to a child is planted in the soil of their heart, quietly shaping how they see themselves, God, and the future. Scripture is clear that the tongue carries power – *the power of life and death (Proverbs 18:21).* What you repeatedly say to a child can either nurture confidence and purpose or produce fear, insecurity, and lasting wounds.

Statements such as "You are useless," "You will never succeed," or "You always fail" do more than express frustration; they assign the wrong identity to the child. Comparison, rejection, and harsh labels imprison a child in a negative self-image that may follow them into adulthood. Even spiritual threats like "God will punish you" distort a child's understanding of a loving Father and replace reverence with fear.

God never corrects His children with condemnation. He disciplines with love, truth, and hope. When parents use words like "I regret giving birth to you" or "I'm tired of you," a child may hear abandonment instead of correction. When they are told to "Shut up," they learn that their voice and feelings do not matter.

These wounds are often invisible, but they are real. However, there is good news: words can also heal. Just as negative words wound, intentional, loving, and faith-filled words can restore what was broken. When parents repent, apologize, and change their language, the Holy Spirit begins a deep healing work in the child's heart. Homes can shift from places of fear to places of affirmation and safety.

Correction is necessary, but correction without condemnation produces strong, secure, and responsible children. Speak truth with love, discipline with dignity, and instruction with hope, and God will redeem even past mistakes.

Action: *Ask God to show you any harmful words you have spoken, apologize to your child, and deliberately speak a blessing over them daily.*

Let us pray

1. *Father, thank You for Your mercy and grace that heals families, in Jesus' name.*
2. *Lord, uproot every negative word spoken over my child and nullify its effects, in Jesus' name.*
3. *Replace every lie planted by harsh words with Your truth and affirmation, in Jesus' name.*
4. *Father, grant me self-control and wisdom to speak life at all times, in Jesus' name.*
5. *Lord, heal my child's heart and restore confidence, joy, and destiny, in Jesus' name.*

Friday 10 April

HOW TO WIN YOUR PARENTS' LOVE

Read: Luke 2:51-52

Bible in 1 year: Rom. 5-8
Bible in 2 years: Mark 9

"Children, obey your parents in the Lord, for this is right. 'Honor your father and mother' - which is the first commandment with a promise" (Ephesians 6:1-2 NIV).

The love of parents is precious, yet relationships between parents and children can sometimes become strained due to misunderstandings, rebellion, or unmet expectations. God's Word offers timeless wisdom on how children, young or grown, can nurture healthy, loving relationships with their parents.

1. ***Honor and Respect Them:*** Honor goes beyond obedience; it includes attitude, tone, and conduct. Even when your parents are imperfect, respectful speech and behavior open their hearts (Proverbs 23:22).
2. ***Practice Obedience and Responsibility:*** Jesus Himself submitted to His earthly parents and grew in favor with God and people (Luke 2:51-52). Responsibility builds trust and strengthens parental affection.
3. ***Communicate With Humility:*** Listening before speaking and expressing yourself without arrogance reduces conflict. Soft answers turn away wrath and invite understanding (Proverbs 15:1).
4. ***Show Appreciation and Gratitude:*** Simple acts of gratitude – words, service, or time affirm parents and

soften strained relationships. Gratitude turns duty into joy.

5. ***Live with Integrity:*** Parents rejoice when their children walk in truth. A godly lifestyle honors them and brings peace to the home (3 John 1:4).

Winning the love of your parents is not about manipulation but alignment with God's principles.

When children walk in honor, humility, and obedience, love grows naturally. Even when relationships are broken, God can restore hearts if we faithfully follow His ways.

Action: *Identify one way you can practically honor your parents this week – through obedience, service, or sincere appreciation, and do it intentionally.*

Let us pray

1. *Father, thank You for the gift of my parents and the role they play in my life, in Jesus' name.*
2. *Lord, give me a humble and obedient heart that honors my parents, in Jesus' name.*
3. *Heal every misunderstanding or wound between my parents and me, in Jesus' name.*
4. *Teach me to communicate with wisdom, respect, and love, in Jesus' name.*
5. *Let peace, unity, and affection reign in our family relationships, in Jesus' name.*

Saturday 11 April

HOW TO REKINDLE LOVE IN YOUR MARRIAGE

Read: Revelation 2:4-5

Bible in 1 year: Rom. 9-11
Bible in 2 years: Mark 10

"Husbands, love your wives, just as Christ loved the church and gave Himself up for her" (Ephesians 5:25, NIV).

Love in marriage is not sustained by feelings alone; it is sustained by intentional choices. Over time, pressure from work, finances, children, ministry, or unresolved conflict can slowly quench the flame of love in your marriage.

Jesus' words to the church in Revelation – *"You have left your first love,"* also speak powerfully to marriage. Love can fade, but it can also be restored. These are the steps to follow:

1. ***Return to Your First Love Practices:*** Remember what you did at the beginning – kind words, quality time, thoughtful gestures. Love grows where attention is given (Song of Songs 2:15).
2. ***Forgive Quickly:*** Unresolved offenses harden hearts and block intimacy. Forgiveness is not denial of pain but a decision to release the debt (Colossians 3:13). Choose to forgive!
3. ***Communicate With Grace:*** Speak honestly, but gently. Listening without interrupting and responding without anger rebuilds emotional connection (James 1:19).

4. ***Prioritize Intimacy and Companionship:*** Emotional closeness and physical intimacy are gifts from God meant to strengthen the marital bond (1 Corinthians 7:3-5).
5. ***Invite God Back into the Center:*** Prayer, shared devotion, and spiritual unity realign hearts. A cord of three strands is not quickly broken (Ecclesiastes 4:12).

Rekindling love in your marriage is not about recreating your past but renewing commitment in your present. If you humble yourself, return to God's design, and act in love even when your feelings are weak, the fire of love will begin to burn again – stronger and purer.

Action: *This week, intentionally do one loving act each day – words, time, or service that reflects how you treated your spouse at the beginning of your marriage.*

Let us pray

1. *Father, thank You for the gift of my spouse and our marriage covenant, in Jesus' name.*
2. *Lord, heal every wound and remove every wall that has cooled our love, in Jesus' name.*
3. *Restore affection, joy, and emotional intimacy in our marriage, in Jesus' name.*
4. *O Lord, help us to forgive quickly and love sacrificially as Christ loves, in Jesus' name.*
5. *Father, let Your presence renew our hearts and strengthen our bond, in Jesus' name.*

Sunday 12 April

STEPS TO GENUINE FAMILY RECONCILIATION

Read: Colossians 3:12-15

Bible in 1 year: Rom. 12-16

Bible in 2 years: Mark 11; 12:1-27

"If it is possible, as far as it depends on you, live at peace with everyone" (Romans 12:18 NIV).

Family reconciliation is not the absence of conflict but the restoration of love, trust, and peace after conflict. Many families remain divided, not because reconciliation is impossible, but because pride, silence, or unresolved wounds are allowed to linger. God's heart is always toward reconciliation, for He Himself reconciled us to Himself through Christ (2 Corinthians 5:18).

Follow these steps to bring reconciliation:

1. ***Acknowledge the Pain Honestly:*** True reconciliation begins when hurt is named, not denied. Healing cannot occur where pain is ignored. Speaking the truth in love opens the door to restoration (Ephesians 4:15).
2. ***Take Responsibility for Your Part:*** Reconciliation does not require one person to be entirely wrong. It takes two people to have a quarrel. Whenever two people quarrel, both are wrong to an extent. Humility is demonstrated when we own our words, attitudes, or actions without excuses (Matthew 7:3-5).
3. ***Forgive Deliberately and Immediately:*** Forgiveness is not a feeling but a decision to release the offense to God. Without forgiveness, reconciliation remains shallow and temporary (Colossians 3:13).

4. ***Restore Communication With Grace:*** Rebuilding trust requires patient, respectful dialogue. Listening attentively and responding gently helps rebuild broken bridges (Proverbs 15:1).
5. ***Commit to Peace and New Patterns:*** Reconciliation is sustained by changed behavior. Families must agree to new boundaries, healthier communication, and continued prayer (Psalm 34:14).

Genuine reconciliation is a process, not an event. It may take time, tears, and repeated acts of humility. But when families pursue peace God's way, He heals wounds, restores relationships, and transforms broken homes into testimonies of grace.

Action: *Prayerfully reach out to one family member this week with a sincere apology, a listening ear, or an offer to reconcile.*

Let us pray

1. *Father, thank You for reconciling us to Yourself through Christ, in Jesus' name.*
2. *Lord, soften our hearts and remove pride, bitterness, and resentment from our family, in Jesus' name.*
3. *Father, give us grace to forgive as we have been forgiven, in Jesus' name.*
4. *O Lord, restore trust, healthy communication, and love among us, in Jesus' name.*
5. *Father, establish lasting peace and unity in our family, in Jesus' name.*

Monday 13 April

UNITE YOUR FAMILY FOR BREAKTHROUGH

Read: Psalm 133:1-3

Bible in 1 year: 2Chron. 1-3
Bible in 2 years: Mark 12:28-44; 13

"Behold, how good and how pleasant it is for brethren to dwell together in unity!" (Psalm 133:1).

Breakthroughs in families are rarely accidental; they are the fruit of unity. God places extraordinary power where hearts agree. Psalm 133 reveals that unity is not merely pleasant; it commands the blessing. When family members walk in harmony, God releases favor, protection, and increase that no individual effort can secure on its own.

Disunity often enters families through unresolved offenses, harsh words, pride, or silence. Small misunderstandings grow into walls, and prayer loses strength where hearts are divided. Jesus taught that a house divided against itself cannot stand (Mark 3:25). The enemy knows this, that is why he targets relationships before resources.

Unity does not mean uniformity or the absence of disagreement; it means choosing love over ego, forgiveness over bitterness, and understanding over accusation. When families decide to reconcile, communicate with grace, and pray together, spiritual alignment is restored. The oil in Psalm 133 flowed from the head to the body. Unity allows God's anointing to reach every member of the family.

Breakthroughs – financial, emotional, spiritual often follow simple acts of unity: eating together, praying together, listening without interrupting, and speaking words that build. As a family, if you submit to God and to one another in love, He will turn your home into an altar of tremendous blessing.

God's desire is not just to bless you as an individual, but to bless your entire family. As you focus on cultivating unity in your family, fear will lose its ground; your prayers will become powerful; and your destinies will experience uncommon progress.

Action: *Call a family meeting as soon as possible to pray together, forgive openly, and agree on one spiritual goal you will pursue as a family.*

Let us pray

1. *Father, thank You for the gift of my family and Your plan to bless us together, in Jesus' name.*
2. *Lord, heal every division, misunderstanding, and offense in our family, in Jesus' name.*
3. *O Lord, bind our hearts together in love, humility, and mutual respect, in Jesus' name.*
4. *Father, let every prayer we pray as a family carry power and bring breakthrough, in Jesus' name.*
5. *Father, command Your blessing – peace, provision, and progress upon our household, in Jesus' name.*

Prophetic Prayers of the Week

1. ***"He teaches my hands to war." (Psalm 144:1).*** *I prevail in every battle that rises against me, in Jesus' name.*
2. ***"The LORD orders the steps of the righteous." (Psalm 37:23).*** *My steps are divinely ordered this week, in Jesus' name.*

3. **"He crowns you with lovingkindness." (Psalm 103:4).** *I am crowned with mercy and compassion, in Jesus' name.*

Tuesday 14 April

TIME TO MOVE TO THE NEXT LEVEL

Read: Deuteronomy 1:2-8

Bible in 1 year: 2Chron. 4-6
Bible in 2 years: Mark 14

"You have stayed long enough at this mountain" (Deuteronomy 1:6).

Many believers sincerely love God, yet they are not living at the level God intends for them – spiritually, professionally, financially, or in purpose.

In Deuteronomy 1, Israel had already experienced deliverance, miracles, and divine guidance. They reached Mount Horeb quickly, but what was meant to be a temporary place of encounter became a prolonged season of delay. Then God spoke clearly and lovingly: *"You have stayed long enough at this mountain. Break camp and advance" (Deuteronomy 1:7).* God was not condemning them; He was calling them forward. He is the God of progress, not stagnation.

Mountains are places of revelation, not destinations. One major reason people stagnate is comfort without progress. Israel grew comfortable when they should have been preparing to move. Scripture warns us, *"Let us go on to maturity" (Hebrews 6:1).* Are you growing? Comfort can feel spiritual, yet it can quietly block destiny. Fear and unbelief also hold people back. Israel saw giants and forgot God's power. Fear often pretends to be wisdom, but it produces delay.

Sometimes, stagnation is reinforced by unseen resistance, but delay does not cancel God's promise.

When your current place no longer stretches you, when God stirs a holy dissatisfaction within your heart, and when He opens your eyes to see more, it is often a sign that your season has shifted. God told Israel, *"See, I have given you the land" (Deuteronomy 1:8).* The promise existed before they moved, but possession required obedience.

A simple illustration makes this clear: a bus stop is useful, but no one builds a house there. Staying too long at a good place can still be disobedience. In Christ, stagnation is not your calling. This is not a season to camp. It is time to move to the next level.

Action: *Prayerfully identify one area where God is calling you to advance and take a deliberate step of obedience this week.*

Let us pray

1. *Father, I thank You for Your patience, guidance, and the promise of growth in my life.*
2. *Lord, uproot every form of stagnation in my spirit, career, and destiny, and move me forward.*
3. *Father, break every fear, unbelief, and comfort zone that has delayed my obedience.*
4. *Lord, remove every visible and invisible resistance standing against my progress.*
5. *Father, empower me through Christ to move by faith and step fully into my next level this year.*

Wednesday 15 April **A NEW ANOINTING FOR ENLARGEMENT**

Read: Isaiah 11:1-3

Bible in 1 year: 2Chron. 7-9
Bible in 2 years: Mark 15

"The Spirit of the LORD will rest on him—the Spirit of wisdom and of understanding, the Spirit of counsel and of might" (Isaiah 11:2).

Enlargement in God's Kingdom is never the product of human strength alone; it is the work of the Holy Spirit. Jesus Christ stands as the perfect example of a life enlarged through divine anointing. Though He was the Son of God, He chose not to operate by self-derived power. Instead, He walked in total dependence on the Spirit, allowing the fullness of God's anointing to shape His wisdom, authority, compassion, and impact. Isaiah 11 reveals that the Spirit rested on Him in fullness, enabling Him to fulfill destiny without strain or compromise.

The anointing is the empowerment of the Holy Spirit released upon a person to accomplish God's assignment. It is not emotion, title, or natural charisma; it is divine enablement. Just as oil reduces friction and allows movement, the anointing removes resistance and enables progress.

This is why Jesus moved with authority, spoke with wisdom, and produced lasting fruit. True enlargement flows from spiritual empowerment, not mere strategy. Isaiah describes the sevenfold Spirit that rested on Christ: the Spirit of the Lord, wisdom, understanding, counsel, might, knowledge, and the fear of the Lord. Each dimension brought balance and expansion. Wisdom gave Him right judgment, understanding gave Him insight beyond information, counsel kept Him aligned with divine timing, might empowered Him to overcome resistance, knowledge deepened His intimacy with the Father, and the fear of the Lord preserved Him in holiness and humility. This fullness ensured that His enlargement was sustained, not seasonal.

The same Spirit is available to believers today. However, new levels of impact require new measures of surrender. Staying connected to Christ, maintaining hunger for the Holy Spirit, and walking in obedience and humility position us to receive fresh anointing. A clean, yielded vessel is always ready for greater use.

As you seek enlargement, remember this truth: when God releases a new anointing, He enlarges your capacity to fulfill destiny and bring glory to His name.

Action: *This week, deepen your walk with Christ through a special time of prayer to seek a fresh infilling of the Holy Spirit.*

Let us pray

1. *Father, I thank You for the gift of the Holy Spirit and for Your power at work in my life.*
2. *Lord, release upon me a fresh anointing that enlarges my capacity to fulfill my divine assignment.*
3. *Holy Spirit, fill me with wisdom, understanding, and counsel to walk accurately in every season.*
4. *Father, clothe me with spiritual might to overcome resistance and break every limitation.*
5. *Lord, preserve me in humility and holiness so that my enlargement will endure and glorify You.*

Thursday 16 April

WALKING IN THE BLESSING

Read: Ephesians 1:3

Bible in 1 year: 2Chron. 10-13

Bible in 2 years: Mark 16, Num. 1:1-27

"The blessing of the LORD makes one rich, and He adds no sorrow with it" (Proverbs 10:22).

Many believers spend their lives praying for blessings without realizing that the blessing is not something we chase; it is a position we walk in. Scripture reveals that blessing is God's divine empowerment resting on a person, enabling them to flourish, grow, and make an impact in accordance with His purpose.

When God blessed Adam in Genesis 1:28, Adam had not yet worked. The blessing came first; labor followed. In Christ, this pattern is restored. Ephesians 1:3 declares that we are already blessed with every spiritual blessing in heavenly places. The issue, therefore, is not whether God has blessed us, but whether we are walking in alignment with that blessing.

It is more than material provision; it is divine capacity. This explains why Joseph prospered even in prison and why Abraham became a blessing wherever he went. The blessing works across seasons. Rain falls everywhere, but only prepared ground produces fruit. In the same way, the blessing flows freely, but its manifestation depends on our posture.

There are clear marks of a blessed life. Divine favor opens doors without manipulation. Supernatural increase brings growth that cannot be explained by effort alone.

Preservation ensures that God's hand covers us in every place and season. Fruitfulness gives visible results that speak louder than words. These are not rewards for perfection; they are outcomes of alignment.

To enjoy the blessing in this year, obedience must be intentional, relationships must be guarded, faith must be active, giving must be practiced, and holiness must be pursued. Sin clogs the flow of blessing just as dirt blocks clean water in a pipe. Wisdom and purity keep the channel open.

As you advance into this year, do not strive anxiously for the blessing. Choose alignment. When you live rightly positioned in Christ, the blessing becomes your atmosphere, and you simply walk in it.

Action: *Is there any domain of your life where you desire a breakthrough? Take time today and really pray about it.*

Let us pray

1. *Father, I thank You for blessing me in Christ and positioning my life under Your divine empowerment for fruitfulness and increase.*
2. *Lord, help me walk in alignment with Your will in 2026, choosing obedience over struggle and faith over fear.*
3. *Holy Spirit, empower me to live wisely and purely, keeping my heart, relationships, and choices in line with Your purpose.*
4. *Father, teach me to live a life of gratitude in every season, opening my heart to receive all You have prepared for me.*
5. *Lord, I declare that in 2026 I walk in favor, increase, protection, and lasting fruitfulness, empowered by Your blessing, in Jesus' name.*

Friday 17 April

PREACH THE WORD IN ALL SEASONS

Read: Luke 9:1-9

Bible in 1 year: Lev. 1-4

Bible in 2 years: Num. 1:28-54; 2

"Preach the word! Be ready in season and out of season. Convince, rebuke, exhort, with all longsuffering and teaching" (2 Timothy 4:2).

The word "gospel" is translated from the Greek word *euaggelion*, which means 'a good message' or 'good news.' It is the announcement to the sinner that Jesus has paid the price for his freedom from sin and its consequences. However, any good news that is not shared is effectively no news at all. If we keep the treasure of salvation to ourselves, those around us may perish in ignorance simply because there was no one to tell them about the love of God.

Jesus made preaching His priority. He didn't just stay in one place; He moved from village to village and sent His disciples out to do the same. Many of us develop strategies of waiting for people to come to our churches, but the Master's strategy was "go." Going out to preach is the cure to the darkness of crime, violence, and witchcraft in our communities. When the light of the Word enters a heart, the darkness must flee.

Have a heart that beats for the lost. We cannot claim to love God whom we cannot see if we do not love our neighbors enough to share the way to eternal life with them. Your testimony, no matter how small, is a powerful weapon against the enemy's lies. Today, decide to be a voice for Christ in your environment.

Action*: Write down the names of three friends or relatives who are not yet saved and begin to pray for their salvation today.*

Let us pray

1. *Father, thank You for the privilege of knowing the truth of Your Word.*
2. *Lord, set my heart on fire with a fresh passion for lost souls.*
3. *Holy Spirit, give me the right words to say when I share the gospel.*
4. *O Lord, break every barrier of fear that stops me from preaching.*
5. *Father, let the gospel I preach be accompanied by signs and wonders.*

Saturday 18 April

WORKING WELL UNDER A DIFFICULT BOSS

Read: Colossians 3:22-24

Bible in 1 year: Lev. 5-7
Bible in 2 years: Num. 3

"Whatever you do, work at it with all your heart, as working for the Lord, not for human masters" (Colossians 3:23 NIV).

Many believers struggle not with the work itself, but with the person they work under. A difficult boss may be harsh, inconsistent, unfair, or unappreciative. Yet Scripture shows that God often uses challenging authority figures as training grounds for destiny, character, and promotion.

Joseph worked faithfully under Potiphar, even though he was a slave and later falsely accused (Genesis 39). His integrity did not immediately change his boss, but it positioned him for divine promotion. God was with Joseph in the system, not outside it.

David served King Saul, a leader driven by jealousy and insecurity. Though Saul mistreated him, David refused to rebel or dishonor him. He said, *"I will not stretch out my hand against the Lord's anointed" (1 Samuel 24:6).* David's restraint preserved his future kingship.

Daniel served under multiple pagan kings, some hostile and unreasonable. Through excellence, wisdom, and prayer, he gained favor, even when policies were unjust (Daniel 6). His respectful firmness and consistency led God to publicly defend him.

These examples teach us that working well under a difficult boss does not mean approving wrongdoing or enduring abuse. It means maintaining integrity, excellence, respect, and prayer while trusting God as the ultimate authority. When we work as unto the Lord, He becomes our defender, promoter, and rewarder.

A difficult boss may delay comfort, but obedience preserves destiny. God sees faithfulness in hidden places and uses it as preparation for greater responsibility. God can use you to change them.

Action: *Decide today to work with excellence and integrity regardless of your boss's attitude, while praying consistently for wisdom and favor.*

Let us pray

1. *Father, thank You for being my true employer and rewarder, in Jesus' name.*
2. *Lord, give me wisdom, patience, and self-control as I work under authority, in Jesus' name.*
3. *Father, help me maintain integrity and excellence even in difficult situations, in Jesus' name.*
4. *Lord, turn every unjust or challenging environment into a platform for growth and favor, in Jesus' name.*
5. *Lord, promote me in Your time and defend me where I cannot defend myself, in Jesus' name.*

Sunday 19 April **GUARD YOUR HEART**

Read: Mark 7:20-23

Bible in 1 year: Lev. 8-10
Bible in 2 years: Num. 4

"Above all else, guard your heart, for everything you do flows from it" (Proverbs 4:23).

Love in the family does not collapse suddenly. It erodes gradually when the heart is left unguarded. Scripture commands us to guard our hearts *above all else* because the heart is the control center of our words, attitudes, reactions, and relationships. Whatever settles in your heart will eventually manifest in your home.

The Hebrew word for *heart* in Proverbs 4:23 is ***'Leb,'*** meaning the inner man – mind, will, emotions, and intentions. To guard the heart is to intentionally protect what influences your thoughts, emotions, and responses. When bitterness, offense, jealousy, suspicion, or unresolved anger enters your heart, love begins to weaken in your home.

Many family conflicts are not caused by major sins but by unguarded hearts. Harsh words spoken in anger, silent grudges, negative assumptions, and unresolved wounds slowly poison love. Paul warns that love *"Keeps no record of wrongs" (1 Corinthians 13:5).* The moment records are kept, intimacy is broken, and trust begins to die. A woman came for counseling with a notebook in which she had recorded every wrong her husband had done to her, supported with pictures.

Guarding your heart does not mean suppressing emotions; it means submitting them to God. Jesus taught that what comes out of a person originates from the heart (Mark 7:21-23). A guarded heart produces patience, kindness, forgiveness, and understanding. An unguarded heart produces strife, coldness, and division.

Joseph guarded his heart even after his brothers betrayed him. Instead of nurturing bitterness, he trusted God. Because his heart remained clean, God used him to restore the very family that wounded him (Genesis 45). A guarded heart preserves destiny.

Homes flourish where hearts are protected through prayer, honest communication, forgiveness, and humility. When the heart is guarded, love is preserved. When love is preserved, the home remains a place of peace.

Action: *Ask God to reveal anything in your heart that threatens love in your home. Deal with it.*

Let us pray

1. *Father, thank You for the gift of my family, in Jesus' name.*
2. *Lord, cleanse my heart from bitterness, offense, and hidden resentment, in Jesus' name.*
3. *Father, help me guard my words, thoughts, and reactions at home, in Jesus' name.*
4. *Father, restore love where it has been weakened by misunderstanding, in Jesus' name.*
5. *Lord, teach us to forgive quickly and love deeply, in Jesus' name.*

Monday 20 April **LOVE GIVES**

Read: 2 Corinthians 9:6-8

Bible in 1 year: Lev. 11-14
Bible in 2 years: Num. 5-6

"For God so loved the world that He gave His only begotten Son…" (John 3:16).

Love is most clearly revealed through giving. If you love, you will give. If you don't give, then you don't love.

The first action Scripture associates with love is not words or emotions, but sacrifice. God so loved… that He gave. Divine love always expresses itself through generosity. Where love is genuine, giving flows naturally.

The world often defines giving by abundance – people give when they feel they have enough. God defines giving by love. He gives even when it costs Him something. Love that does not give is incomplete. That is why families that cultivate generosity experience lasting blessings and peace.

The Greek word for love in John 3:16 is *'Agape,'* meaning unconditional, selfless, sacrificial love. Agape is not driven by convenience or reward; it gives because it cares – it values people. When agape governs a home, stinginess, competition, and selfishness lose their power. Generosity becomes a lifestyle, not an event. It is sad how some couples are stingy towards each other.

Scripture teaches that generosity attracts divine increase. Proverbs 11:24-25 reveals a spiritual paradox: *"There is one who scatters, yet increases more."* God ensures that those who refresh others are themselves refreshed. Families that open their hands never lack God's supply.

Jesus demonstrated this consistently. He fed the hungry, touched the outcast, and gave Himself fully on the cross. The early church followed His example, sharing their resources so that none lacked (Acts 4:32-35). Their generosity released unity, joy, and supernatural provision.

A generous home teaches children compassion, gratitude, and trust in God. It shifts focus from "What do we have?" to "Who can we help?" Such families become channels of God's grace in their communities.

Beloved, love grows when it is shared. Giving does not diminish you; it multiplies you. When love gives, God responds with overflow.

Action: *Intentionally give today – time, kindness, or resources, to bless someone in need.*

Let us pray

1. *Father, thank You for loving me and giving freely to me, in Jesus' name.*
2. *Lord, deliver my heart and my family from selfishness, in Jesus' name.*
3. *Father, teach us to give joyfully and sacrificially, in Jesus' name.*
4. *Father, let generosity become a culture in our home, in Jesus' name.*
5. *Father, help us to use our resources to bless lives and glorify You, in Jesus' name.*

Prophetic Prayers of the Week

1. ***"You shall not die, but live." (Psalm 118:17).*** *I shall live to fulfill God's purpose, in Jesus' name.*

2. **"The righteous shall flourish like a palm tree." (Psalm 92:12).** *I will flourish where God has planted me and bear abundant fruits for His glory, in Jesus' name.*
3. **"The LORD will perfect that which concerns me." (Psalm 138:8).** *My destiny is secured and perfected by God, in Jesus' name.*

Tuesday 21 April

THE PRICE OF TRUE UNITY

Read: John 15:12-14

Bible in 1 year: Lev. 15-16
Bible in 2 years: Num. 7:1-41

"Therefore be imitators of God, as beloved children. And walk in love, as Christ loved us and gave himself up for us, a fragrant offering and sacrifice to God" (Ephesians 5:1-2).

True unity in the family, church, or community does not come by agreement alone. It is sustained by sacrificial love. Unity always costs something. Where people insist on convenience, pride, or personal rights, unity quickly breaks down. But where love is willing to lay something down, unity flourishes.

Jesus defined the highest form of love as SACRIFICE. He did not merely teach unity; He paid for it. On the cross, Christ laid down His life to reconcile us to God and to one another (Ephesians 2:14-16). Unity is preserved when believers choose to put others before themselves, just as Christ did.

The Greek word for love used by Jesus is *'Agape'* – unconditional, self-giving love. Agape does not ask, "WHAT DO I GAIN?" but "WHAT MUST I GIVE?" It sacrifices comfort, time, pride, and sometimes personal preferences to protect relationships. Philippians 2:3-5 calls us to this mindset: esteeming others better than ourselves.

Many families and churches struggle with division because of the absence of sacrifice. Unforgiveness, competition, and self-interest fracture relationships. Yet unity is restored when someone chooses humility over pride, forgiveness over offense, and peace over being right. Sacrificial love always goes first.

Consider Christ washing the disciples' feet (John 13:3-5). Though He was their Lord, He humbled Himself to serve them. That act of sacrifice set the tone for unity among His followers. Unity flows where service replaces status.

Beloved, unity is not sustained by strong personalities but by strong love. When sacrificial love becomes a lifestyle, strife loses its grip, and God commands His blessing to flow (Psalm 133:1-3).

Action: *Choose one way today to sacrifice your comfort to preserve unity.*

Let us pray

1. *Father, thank You for loving me sacrificially through Christ, in Jesus' name.*
2. *Lord, deliver my heart from pride and self-interest, in Jesus' name.*
3. *Father, teach me to love like Jesus – selflessly and humbly, in Jesus' name.*
4. *O Lord, heal every division in my family and relationships, in Jesus' name.*
5. *Father, arise and restore unity in my family and Church, where it has been broken, in Jesus' name.*

Wednesday 22 April **THE SEAL OF OWNERSHIP**

Read: 2 Timothy 2:19;
Ephesians 1:13-14

Bible in 1 year: Lev. 17-19
Bible in 2 years: Num. 7:42-89

"Nevertheless the solid foundation of God stands, having this seal: 'The Lord knows those who are His,' and, 'Let everyone who names the name of Christ depart from iniquity.'" (2 Timothy 2:19)

In ancient times, when a king sent a scroll, he would pour hot wax on the seam and press his signet ring into it. This "seal" served two purposes: it proved ownership, and it guaranteed protection. Anyone who broke that seal answered to the king's entire army. Holiness is the visible "seal" of God upon your life. It is the evidence that you no longer belong to yourself or to the kingdom of darkness. God expects you to carry the "mark" of the King so clearly that the enemy recognizes he has no legal right to touch the goods.

The seal has two sides. One side says, "The Lord knows those who are His"—that is God's commitment to you. The other side says, "Depart from iniquity"—that is your commitment to God. You cannot claim the protection of the seal while ignoring the command of the seal. When you "name the name of Christ" but continue to live in secret sin, the seal becomes blurred, and the enemy finds a loophole to attack. But when you live a life of separation, your "ownership" is undisputed in the spirit realm.

Being "sealed" means you are "off the market." You

are no longer available for the world's use, for the devil's manipulation, or for the flesh's whims. You are a "private property" of Heaven. This realization should give you great confidence. If God owns you, God protects you. If God owns you, God provides for you. Today, take pride in the "seal" of holiness. Don't see "departing from iniquity" as a loss of freedom, but as the activation of your divine insurance policy.

Prophetic Declaration: *I am sealed by God! I belong to the King! I am off-limits to the kingdom of darkness!*

Let us pray

1. *Father, I thank You for sealing me with Your Holy Spirit of promise.*
2. *Lord, let the seal of Your ownership be visible in my character and conduct today.*
3. *Lord, give me the strength to depart from every form of iniquity, seen and unseen.*
4. *Father, I declare that I am Your private property; no enemy has a right to my life.*
5. *Holy Spirit, keep the mark of Christ fresh and clear upon my heart.*

Thursday 23 April

GIVE WITH LOVE AND HUMILITY

Read: 2 Corinthians 8:1-5

Bible in 1 year: Lev. 20-23
Bible in 2 years: Num. 8-9

"And do not forget to do good and to share with others, for with such sacrifices God is pleased" (Hebrews 13:16 NIV).

Christian giving is not measured first by amounts but by motives. Scripture reveals that liberality and simplicity flow most purely from love, not from abundance. Paul testifies that the Macedonian believers, though in "extreme poverty," overflowed in rich generosity because they first gave themselves to the Lord (2 Corinthians 8:2-5). Possessions did not possess them; love did.

The New Testament often uses *'Haplotes'* to mean "generosity," "singleness," or "simplicity of heart." It describes giving without mixed motives – no pride, no show. Humility is *'Tapeinophrosyne,'* a lowliness of mind that places God and people above self. When generosity flows from humility, heaven is pleased.

Jesus once highlighted a poor widow whose offering seemed insignificant to others but was precious to God because it came from her whole heart. This reveals a profound truth: the more some people accumulate, the tighter fear grips their hearts. Money is a wonderful servant but a terrible master.

A small village church once gathered an offering for flood victims. One elderly woman brought eggs from her farm, the only resource she had. Those eggs fed families that night. Her gift preached louder than any large cheque because it was wrapped in love.

John Wesley wisely warned, "When I have money, I get rid of it quickly, lest it find a way into my heart." God Himself models pure generosity. He values people above possessions and gives to restore the broken. When love drives giving, generosity becomes a channel of rescue and revelation.

Give, not to impress people, but to please God. Give with love and humility, and you will harvest eternal blessings.

Action: *This week, give intentionally to someone in need with no desire for recognition.*

Let us pray

1. *Father, thank You for Your generous love and for every opportunity You give me to share, in Jesus' name.*
2. *Lord, purify my motives and deliver me from pride and selfishness, in Jesus' name.*
3. *Father, help me to value people above possessions and eternity above applause, in Jesus' name.*
4. *Lord, make my resources a channel of blessing and restoration to others, in Jesus' name.*
5. *Lord, teach me to give consistently with love, humility, and joy, in Jesus' name.*

Read: Matthew 10:28-31

Bible in 1 year: Lev. 24-27
Bible in 2 years: Num. 10-11

"So God created man in His own image; in the image of God He created him; male and female He created them" (Genesis 1:27).

Human life is sacred because it originates from God. From the beginning, Scripture reveals that every human being carries divine value, not because of wealth, intelligence, tribe, gender, age, or achievement, but because humanity is created in God's image. To value life is to honor God's love expressed through creation.

The Hebrew word for image in Genesis 1:27 is *'Tselem,'* meaning a representation or reflection. This means every person reflects something of God's nature and glory. When we demean, abuse, neglect, or dehumanize others, we are not merely hurting people, we are dishonoring God Himself.

Jesus consistently demonstrated the divine value of human life. He touched lepers, welcomed children, defended the woman caught in adultery, and ate with those society rejected. In Matthew 10:30-31, Jesus reminds us that even the hairs of our heads are numbered. If God values human life with such detail, then love demands that we do the same.

Many homes, communities, and nations suffer because human life is cheapened – through violence, injustice, neglect, and indifference. Yet divine love calls us to see people through God's eyes. Love does not exploit; it protects. Love does not destroy; it preserves. Love does not discard; it restores.

Valuing human life begins at home. The words you speak to your spouse, children, and relatives either affirm their worth or crush their identity. A home filled with love becomes a place where dignity is restored, confidence is nurtured, and purpose is awakened. When life is valued, love flourishes.

The cross is the ultimate proof of God's value for human life. JESUS DID NOT DIE FOR PROPERTY OR SYSTEMS, HE DIED FOR PEOPLE. Every life is worth the blood of Christ. That truth should reshape how we speak, act, forgive, and serve others.

Beloved, when you value life, you reflect divine love. When you protect dignity, God entrusts you with influence. Love that values life invites heaven's approval.

Action: *Decide today to speak only words that affirm the worth and dignity of those around you.*

Let us pray

1. *Father, thank You for creating every human life with purpose and value, in Jesus' name.*
2. *Lord, help me see people through Your eyes of love, in Jesus' name.*
3. *Father, deliver me from words or attitudes that diminish human dignity, in Jesus' name.*
4. *Lord, heal every wound in me caused by rejection, abuse, or neglect, in Jesus' name.*
5. *Father, make my home a place where life is honored, and love is expressed in Jesus' name.*

Saturday 25 April

SAFEGUARD YOUR EYES AND MIND

Read: Matthew 6:22-23

Bible in 1 year: Luke 1-3
Bible in 2 years: Num. 12-13

"I will set nothing wicked before my eyes; I hate the work of those who fall away; it shall not cling to me" (Psalm 101:3).

The strength of your purity depends on how faithfully you guard your eyes. Sadly, David's downfall began with a look (2 Samuel 11). His eyes lingered on what he should have turned away from. This reminds us that the eye is not just a physical organ; it is a gateway to the soul. What enters through your eyes often shapes your thoughts, fuels your desires, and influences your actions.

The Greek word for "good," *'haplous,'* in Matthew 6:22 means "single, clear, or undivided." A healthy eye is one fixed on God, undistracted by sin or worldly allurements. But when the eyes wander, the mind is soon entangled.

Our generation is flooded with images and distractions from media, advertising, and entertainment, all competing for our attention. Without discipline, your eyes can become doors through which impurity and temptation enter, polluting your mind and weakening your will.

Just as a computer infected with a virus slows down and malfunctions, so too does the mind when it receives corrupt input. Guarding the eyes is like installing strong antivirus protection; it filters what enters, so the system stays strong.

Safeguarding your eyes and mind requires intentional choices: avoiding harmful sights, filtering what you watch, memorizing Scripture, and allowing the Spirit to renew your thoughts (Romans 12:2). When your eyes are fixed on Christ, your heart remains aligned with His light.

Action: *Are there images or videos on your phone you need to remove? Take a decisive step by deleting them and blocking the websites and apps that draw your heart toward sin*

Let us pray

1. *Father, thank You for the power of the Holy Spirit at work in my body, soul, and spirit.*
2. *O Father, let Your fire set my eyes and mind free from anything that corrupts my soul, in Jesus' name.*
3. *Place your hand on your head and pray 5 times, "I receive the blood of Jesus in my mind for the purification of every evil thought, in Jesus' name."*
4. *I receive the grace to fix my gaze on Christ and heavenly realities, in Jesus' name.*
5. *Father, deliver me from the spirit of distraction and lust, and fill my heart with the fire of holiness, in Jesus' name.*

Sunday 26 April

LESSONS FROM GEHAZI'S FALL

Read: 2 Kings 5:20-27

Bible in 1 year: Luke 4-6
Bible in 2 years: Num. 14

"For the love of money is a root of all kinds of evil. Some people, eager for money, have wandered from the faith and pierced themselves with many griefs" (1 Timothy 6:10 NIV).

The story of Gehazi is not just about greed; it is a warning to every servant of God about misplaced priority. Elisha had just demonstrated God's grace by freely healing Naaman, proving that salvation and blessing are not commodities for sale. Yet Gehazi, blinded by greed, secretly pursued the Syrian General to demand payment. His act of covetousness led to the loss of his ministry, the anointing, and his health.

The Hebrew word for "greed," *'Batsa,'* carries the sense of unjust gain, cutting off others to seize what is not yours. Gehazi's heart was cut off from truth because he lusted for wealth outside of God's will. In contrast, Jesus warned in Matthew 6:24 that no one can serve two masters: you cannot serve both God and money (*mammon* in Greek, meaning wealth personified as an idol). Gehazi attempted to serve both, but ended up a servant of shame – bearing the leprosy of Naaman.

A missionary once testified that he was offered a fortune to dilute the gospel message for political acceptance. He refused, saying, "I would rather remain poor in the eyes of men than bankrupt in the eyes of God." That is the spirit Gehazi lacked.

Here are some lessons from Gehazi's fall:

1. Guard your heart because hidden greed will eventually manifest.
2. Value God's presence above possessions. The anointing is priceless.
3. Remember the next generation when you act. Gehazi's sin cursed his descendants.
4. Choose contentment. True wealth is godliness with contentment (1 Timothy 6:6).

Action: *Spend this day searching your heart before God to deal with greed and stinginess.*

Let us pray

1. *Father, I thank You for warning me through Gehazi's story, in Jesus' name.*
2. *Lord, deliver me from every hidden love of money, in Jesus' name.*
3. *O Father, let integrity and purity guide my ministry, in Jesus' name.*
4. *Merciful Father, never allow me to do something that will activate a generational curse on my children, in Jesus' name.*
5. *Fire of God, fall in our Church and deliver Your servants from the spirit of Gehazi, in Jesus' name.*

Monday 27 April

5 WAYS IMMORALITY DESTROYS A DESTINY

Read: Proverbs 5:1-14

Bible in 1 year: Luke 7-9
Bible in 2 years: Num. 15

"Flee also youthful lusts: but follow righteousness, faith, charity, peace, with them that call on the Lord out of a pure heart" (2 Timothy 2:22).

Your destiny is God's ordained purpose for your life. It is precious and powerful. Hence, Scripture repeatedly warns that immorality has a unique capacity to derail or destroy your destiny if not confronted early and decisively. God's warnings are not to restrict joy, but to protect purpose.

Here are five ways immorality can destroy your destiny:

1. ***It Weakens Your Spiritual Sensitivity:*** Immorality dulls the conscience and grieves the Holy Spirit, making it harder to hear God's voice and respond to His direction (Ephesians 4:30).
2. ***It Drains Strength And Focus:*** Proverbs warns that immoral living gives one's strength to others. Time, energy, and passion meant for purpose are consumed by guilt, secrecy, and distraction.
3. ***It Damages Reputation And Trust:*** Destiny often requires credibility. Immorality erodes trust with family, mentors, and communities, closing doors God intended to open.

4. ***It Creates Cycles of Bondage:*** What begins as a choice can become a habit. Bondage limits freedom, delays growth, and keeps a person circling the same battles instead of advancing.
5. ***It Invites Painful Consequences That Outlive The Moment:*** Scripture says wounds and dishonor remain (Proverbs 6:33). Even when forgiven, consequences can affect relationships, opportunities, and confidence.

But there is hope. God can restore you if you sincerely repent. He will cleanse, heal, and realign your destiny when you turn back to Him with humility. Joseph fled immorality and stepped into leadership; Samson toyed with it and lost his strength. The difference was not in their calling, but in their choices.

Destiny is preserved by obedience. Holiness is not weakness; it is wisdom that protects tomorrow. *"How can a young person stay on the path of purity? By living according to Your word"* (Psalm 119:9).

Action: *Identify one area where you must set firmer boundaries today against immorality, and take action to protect your destiny.*

Let us pray

1. *Father, I thank You for Your grace, mercy, and protection over my life and my family.*
2. *Lord, I receive strength from You to flee every form of sexual immorality and hidden compromise.*
3. *Holy Spirit, cleanse my heart, mind, and body, and empower me to walk in purity daily.*
4. *Father, grant me victory over temptation and discipline to guard my eyes, thoughts, and desires.*
5. *Lord, establish holiness in my life and let my choices protect my family and future generations*

Prophetic Prayers of the Week

1. ***"The joy of the LORD is your strength." (Nehemiah 8:10).*** *I am strengthened daily by the joy of the Lord, in Jesus' name.*
2. ***"The Lord is a shield around me." (Psalm 3:3).*** *I am divinely defended on every side, in Jesus' name.*
3. ***"He restores my soul." (Psalm 23:3). My soul*** *is restored and refreshed today, in Jesus' name.*

Read: Proverbs 10:9

Bible in 1 year: Luke 10-13
Bible in 2 years: Num. 16

"The righteous man walks in his integrity; his children are blessed after him" (Proverbs 20:7).

Integrity is one of the greatest treasures you can possess as a believer. Integrity is the key to prosperity, security, and longevity.

The Hebrew word for "Integrity" is *'Tom,'* meaning "Completeness, innocence, and sincerity." It paints the picture of someone whose life is whole, consistent, and without hidden faults. To walk in integrity is to live the same in private as in public.

The Bible emphasizes that your character is greater than wealth. *"Better is the poor who walks in his integrity than one who is crooked in his ways, though he be rich" (Proverbs 28:6).* God values your honesty and reliability above your success or talent.

Billy Graham once said, "When wealth is lost, nothing is lost; when health is lost, something is lost; when character is lost, everything is lost." This statement remains a profound reminder that integrity is the bedrock of leadership and legacy.

Reflect on this businessman who refused a bribe even though it meant losing a lucrative contract. He was mocked at the time, but years later, his integrity gave him influence as a trusted consultant for government leaders. His decision blessed not only himself but also his family.

Integrity guarantees generational blessing. God Himself promises that the children of a righteous person are blessed after him (Proverbs 20:7). By living with integrity, you are writing the history your children will inherit.

Choose daily to be truthful, faithful, and dependable. Even if no one else notices, God sees, and heaven records. Integrity may cost you in the short term, but it always brings eternal reward.

Action: *Is there an area of your life in which God wants you to exercise integrity? Decide now to do it?*

Let us pray

1. *Thank You, Lord, for calling me to walk in integrity, in Jesus' name.*
2. *Father, deliver me from compromise and double standards, in Jesus' name.*
3. *Lord, strengthen me to live consistently before You and men, in Jesus' name.*
4. *Father, let my life be a testimony of righteousness in my workplace, in Jesus' name.*
5. *Father, cause my children inherit the blessings of integrity, in Jesus' name.*

Wednesday 29 April **VICTORY OVER TEMPTATION**

Read: 1 Corinthians 10:13

Bible in 1 year: Luke 14-17
Bible in 2 years: Num. 17-18

"For we do not have a High Priest who cannot sympathize with our weaknesses, but was in all points tempted as we are, yet without sin" (Hebrews 4:15).

Temptation is a universal experience, but victory is guaranteed through Christ. The Greek word for "Temptation" in 1 Corinthians 10:13 is '*Peirasmos,*' meaning "A test, trial, or enticement to sin." This shows that temptation is not sin itself; it is an invitation we can either accept or reject.

Jesus Himself was tempted in the wilderness (Matthew 4:1-11). Yet He overcame by standing on the Word: *"It is written."* This proves that the Word of God is our sword of victory over temptation (Ephesians 6:17).

An old preacher once said, "You can't stop birds from flying over your head, but you can stop them from building a nest there." Similarly, you may not prevent temptation from coming, but you can refuse to entertain it.

I recall counseling a young man struggling with pornography. His turning point came when he began memorizing and declaring Scriptures whenever temptation struck. The Word of God began to renew his mind and weaken the stronghold of sin. Today, he testifies of lasting freedom.

Jesus understands our weaknesses and intercedes for us daily (Hebrews 7:25). Because He overcame, we too can overcome. We do not fight in our strength, but by His Spirit (Zechariah 4:6). Surround yourself with godly accountability, saturate your heart with Scripture, and lean on prayer.

Victory over temptation is possible, not by willpower but by Christ's power.

Action: *Are you feeling pressured to compromise? Seek help now—before the fall, not after it.*

Let us pray

1. *Thank You, Lord, for providing a way of escape in every temptation, in Jesus' name.*
2. *Lord, give me strength to resist the schemes of the enemy, in Jesus' name.*
3. *Father, fill my heart with Your Word as a shield, in Jesus' name.*
4. *O Lord, surround me with godly influences that build holiness, in Jesus' name.*
5. *I overcome temptation by the blood of Jesus and the power of His Word, and sin shall not have dominion over me, in Jesus' name.*

Thursday 30 April **LIVE EVERY DAY PREPARED**

Read: Matthew 24:37-44

Bible in 1 year: Luke 18-21
Bible in 2 years: (Catch-up)

"He will keep you strong to the end so that you will be free from all blame on the day when our Lord Jesus Christ returns" (1 Corinthians 1:8 NLT).

Are you prepared to stand before God in judgment? Many people, even some Christians, live as though they will never give an account of their lives. The Holy Spirit invites us today to reflect seriously on eternity. Years ago, a young man said, *"When I grow, get married, and enjoy life to the fullest, then I will consider accepting Jesus."* He sounded confident, but his words revealed deep ignorance about the uncertainty of life and the danger of dying without Christ. Preparation for eternity is not something to postpone.

In Matthew 24:37-44, Jesus compares His return to the days of Noah. People were eating, drinking, marrying, and carrying on with life, until judgment suddenly came. They were not wicked because they worked or celebrated; they were unprepared because they ignored God's warning.

Jesus emphasizes that His return will be sudden and unexpected. Therefore, He commands, *"Be ready."* Readiness is not fear-driven panic; it is a lifestyle of faithfulness.

Paul explains how believers can remain ready. God Himself is at work, strengthening us and preserving us blameless until the day of Christ (1 Corinthians 1:8). Readiness is not achieved by human effort alone but by daily dependence on

God's grace. As we walk with Christ, He shapes our character, convicts us of sin, and empowers us to live holy lives.

Practically, remaining ready means living with eternity in view. It involves daily repentance, obedience to God's Word, faithfulness in prayer, and love for others. It also means refusing spiritual complacency and keeping our hearts sensitive to the Holy Spirit. Prepared believers do not merely wait for Christ; they live in a way that honors Him.

Action: *Examine your life today. Remove anything that dulls your spiritual alertness, and renew your commitment to live each day ready to meet the Lord.*

Let us pray

1. *Lord, awaken my heart to live daily with eternity in view, in Jesus' name.*
2. *Father, cleanse me from every sin that makes me unprepared for Christ's return, in Jesus' name.*
3. *Holy Spirit, strengthen me to remain faithful and watchful until the end, in Jesus' name.*
4. *Lord, help me to walk in obedience and holiness as I await Your coming, in Jesus' name.*
5. *Father, keep me blameless and ready for the day I meet Jesus Christ, in Jesus' name.*

WHAT YOUR SUPPORT WILL DO

It is very clear through the numerous miracles, breakthroughs and transformation of lives that God has chosen to use this ministry to stir a revival among His people in Cameroon and beyond. I received the call alone but I cannot execute it alone. You have a unique role to play in this divine project. Join us as we take the Gospel to every corner of Cameroon and beyond.

We want to start placing copies of this book in hotels, hospitals, schools and homes, to touch the lives of people with the gospel of Jesus Christ. Just as you have been blessed by this book, they too will be mightily blessed.

TESTIMONY

Every month, hundreds of copies of this Prayer Storm Daily Prayer Guide are distributed freely, thanks to the kind gesture of our partners. May God bless all of you who faithfully sponsor this outreach through your financial seed. You too can sponsor 10, 25, 50, 100 or even more copies to be printed and distributed charge-free to those who are hungry for the word.

Call the numbers: (237) 699.90.26.18 or 674.49.58.95 send an email to voiceofrevivalcameroon@yahoo.com.

If you want to become a distributor of our literature, contact us directly and we will give you the directives on how to do so.

WHERE TO BUY THIS PRAYER GUIDE

<u>CRN Centres</u>

- **Yaounde:** ***Prayer Storm Headquarters:*** 1st Floor Storey Building at Entrée Lycée de Tsinga village on the edge of the main road. **Contact:** 681.72.24.04/ 696.56.58.64
- **Bamenda:** Revival Christian Book Center, **Cow Street**: 675.14.04.50/ 694.20.04.51
- **Douala/PK 8:** All American Depot opposite Lycée **Cité des Palmiers**: 678.04.11.41/ 696.90.76.09/ 670.34.42.32

<u>Adamawa</u>

- **Banyo:** FGM: 677.92.05.98/ 674.64.71.31
- **Meinganga:** EEL: 699.65.02.67/ 652.70.40.68
- **Ngaoundere:** EEC Mont des Oliviers: 674.14.20.51, EEL: 690.06.37.14
- **Tibati:** EEC: 681.01.33.34

<u>Centre</u>

- **Eseka:** FGM: 675.07.56.24
- **Mbalmayo:** EEC: 675.12.86.85/
- **Mfou:** FGM: 677.36.43.28
- **Monatelé:** FGM: 677.58.42.99
- **Yaounde:** EEC **Biyem-assi**: 675.61.86.00/ 677.49.95.83/ 691.26.18.08, EEC **Nlongkak**: 677.56.41.09, EEC **Nouvelle Alliance**: 670.80.56.93, FGM **Biyem-assi**: 675.14.72.70, FGM **Etoug-Ebé**: 671.47.75.78/ 673.50.42.33, Galaxy Computers, Châteaux **Ngoa-Ekelle**: 670.52.75.26, **Yaounde: Librairie Chrétienne** Les Champions op. Total Caveau, **Mvog-Ada**: 675.51.02.86, **LC Maison de la Grâce**, Montée Jouvence op. Olympia: 675.38.46.96, **LC Maison de la**

Bénédiction, Marché Nsam: 691.64.47.84, **LC la Rhema**, Marché Essos, Terminus: 679.39.37.42, **LC Maison du Salut**, Pharmacie du Soleil, Carrefour MEEC: 674.85.16.33/ 699.33.85.11, **LC Livre de Vie**, Mini ferme: 675.00.45.60, **LC Bethesda**, Tsinga: 679.97.06.26, **Overcomers Christian Bookshop**, op. Djongolo Hospital, EtoaMeki: 677.16.46.20, **Mount Zion Christian Bookshop**, op. SONEL TKC: 663.25.86.23 / 675.21.94.35, **Tongolo**: 675.62.86.00, **Olembe**: 651.63.52.34, **DGI-Carrefour Abbia** 652.22.22.49, **Messassi**: 675.24.70.73, **Nkozoa**: 670.29.50.18, **Essos**: 677.53.94.52, **Odzja**: 679.97.47.08, **Etoug-Ebé**: 675.37.18.11, **Mimboman**: 699.90.52.84, **Poste Centrale**: 650.70.08.07, **Emombo**: 699.90.52.84, **Lycée Emana**: 677.86.23.14

East

- **Batouri:** FGM: 664.86.41.80
- **Bertoua:** CBC, **quartier Ngaikada** ou **Aprilé centrale** sous-préfecture: 678.00.63.20/ 694.25.69.20, Collège Bilingue de l'Orient, entrée Hôpital Régionale, **quartier Italy**: 670.56.81.49, FGM, **Nkolbikon**: 696.57.95.43, 677.65.46.76, FGM, **Tigaza**: 674.15.13.18
- **Yokadouma:** FGM: 673.16.24.95/ 696.51.73.70

Far-North

- **Maroua:** Église Missionnaire du Réveil (EMIR) **Baoliwop**: 694.43.33.63, FGM **Harde**: 675.33.12.27, Roman Catholic Church: 673.15.19.76
- **Yagoua:** FGM: 675.691.869

Littoral

Douala: Dakar: La Gloire Phone, immeuble X Tigi, Commissariat 11e: 697.60.57.85, **Kotto:** Behind Neptune fuel station, **Bloc M:** 677.68.18.52, **Bonaberi:** 677.89.87.46, **Akwa:** 691.04.14.59/ 677.91.29.45, **Logpom:** 677.68.18.52/ 651.78.57.30, **Carrefour Lycée de Maképé:** 698.09.42.63, **PK 12 (Marché):** 677.91.29.45/ 696.13.99.26, **Texaco-Nkoulouluon:** 675.18.79.85/695112610 691.04.14.59, **Terminus Saint Michel :** 675187985, La Gloire Phone, Maison X. Tigi, **Carrefour entrée Bille:** 678.19.90.85, **PK 21:** 670.79.05.40/ 691.04.14.59, **Bonanjo:** 691.04.14.59, 677061705 691.04.14.59, **Ange Raphael ESSEC:** 694.26.12.28/ 677.91.29.45, 698360441, **Bonamoussadi Maetur:** 694.26.12.28/ 677.91.29.45, **Village:** 670.79.05.40/ 691.04.14.5, Sure Foundation **Bonabéri:** Ancienne route op. Lycée de Bonaberi Winners Chapel: 671.403.761

- **Nkongsamba:** FGM: 676.40.90.55
- **Melong - GCEPAL:** Tel: 677.80.16.45

North

- **Garoua:** FGM: 678.67.04.22/ 699.91.91.65

North-West

- **Bamenda:** Bamenda Main Market, **Shed 15**: 679.45.11.88, Carmel Cooperative Credit Union (CarCCUL), **Sonac Street**/Tél: 651.04.21.27, FGM NW1 Area office, opposite Garanti Express: 679.46.63.31, FGM, **Cow Street**: 677.21.97.22, FGM, **Mbomassa**: 683.40.40.88, Omega Fire Ministry, **Foncha junction**: 677.93.19.98, ACADI head office, **Wakiki junction**: 672.82.77.84, SUMAN Christian Book Center, **Sonac Street**: 675.72.91.32/ 665.49.98.48, Victory Computers, Food market, **Fishpond hill**: 677.64.19.54, Wailing Women: 696.00.35.07/ 674.57.36.76

- **Batibo:** FGM: 677.31.25.45
- **Njinikom/Mbingo:** BERUDA: 677.60.14.07
- **Jakiri:** FGM, **Nkar**: 677.73.82.91
- **Kumbo:** FGM: 675.72.91.32
- **Mbengwi:** FGM: 677.33.73.86
- **Ndop:** Bruno Bijouterie, Central park: 674.97.59.34
- **Wum:** FGM Central Town: 677.64.32.56, PCC Kesu: 677.13.83.51

West

- **Bafang:** FGM, **Bafang**: 655.00.25.57
- **Bafia:** FGM: 675.21.92.95/ 695.54.96.14
- **Bafoussam:** Alliance biblique du Cameroun, **Tamdja**, SOREPCO: 699.74.79.10, Radio Bonne Nouvelle: 699.93.09.32, Librairie chrétienne du **Camp** oignon: 699.51.47.25, LC PAROLE DE VIE, **gare routière de** Ndiangdam: 699.75.50.99, Dépôt RAYON AMBIANCE **marché A**: 699.42.78.47, EEC **Tamdja**: 696.14.90.16, EEC **Kamkop**: 699.44.03.59, EEC **Plateau**: 696.17.54.23, EEC **Toket**: 695.56.43.61, EEC **SOCADA**: 697.85.65.65, EEC **Tyo-Baleng**: 670.89.70.52, EEC **Kouogouo**: 675.42.27.86, EEC **Diangdam**: 698.35.20.37, FGM **Kamkop**: 653.83.11.80, Faith Bible Church: 683.94.01.21
- **Baham:** FGM: 677.47.55.79
- **Bandjoun:** FGM: 676.41.49.09
- **Bangangte:** EEC **Banekane**: 677.86.47.68
- **Banyo:** FGM: 677.92.05.98/ 674.64.71.31
- **Dschang:** FGM: 675.18.79.85/ 656.20.07.02, FGM **Minmeto**: 681.08.78.37/ 655.01.81.09

- **Foumban:** Décoration Splendeur, **CAMOCO**/Tel.: 677.79.30.83/ 694.85.09.25
- **Kombou:** EEC: 675.81.36.07
- **Mbouda:** FGM: 696.10.41.33/ 676.36.18.11, Cyber Café Pressing near Espace Saint Pierre du Fossie, op. Party House: 675.00.91.15, EEC **Mbouda Centre**: 695.61.97.79

South

- **Ebolowa:** FGM: 677.66.00.19/ 671.90.97.22
- **Kribi:** Carrefour Django: 675.957.912
- **Kye-Ossi:** FGM: 678.78.00.90/ 699.95.96.99

South-West

- **Buea:** FGM **Molyko**: 677.86.47.68, Molyko, near Express Union, **Check Point**: 675.06.37.78,
- **Ekona:** FGM: 675.84.26.91
- **Kumba:** Caisse Populaire Coopérative Carmel (CarCCUL), **Sonac Street**: 675.45.12.21, Glorious Christian Book Center, **Sonac Street**: 677.62.58.49
- **Lebialem:** FGM de **Talung**, Bamumbu – Wabane: 670.466.121
- **Limbe:** Librairie Amen, **New town**: 677.16.51.62, FGM **Mawoh**: 675.78.94.19, FGM **Cow Fence**: 675.73.20.02
- **Misaje:** Kingdom Restoration Parish (KRP) **opposite the hospital**: 679.33.66.53
- **Mutengene:** FGM: 675.36.36.84
- **Muyuka:** FGM: 673.428.985, Royal Priesthood Nursery and Primary School: 677.72.76.80
- **Tiko:** FGM: 654.88.75.57, 674.47.34.36
- **Tombel:** Baptist Church Waterfall: 677.92.33.58

ABROAD:

- **N'Djamena (Chad):** Evang. Kaltouma Aguidi: (235) 95.01.99.92
- **Libreville (Gabon):** Rev. Petipa Flaubert: (241) 05.31.27.39

Pay for your book orders (DISTRIBUTORS ONLY) at:
EcoBank, Acc. No: 0200212620638901 **or** ORANGE Mobile Money, Acc. No: 696880058
Info lines: (237) 677436964, 675686005, 673571953, 679465717;
crnprayerstorm@gmail.com,
prayerstorm@christianrestorationnetwork.org,
www.christianrestorationnetwork.org

Send Financial Support to: ECOBANK Bamenda Acc. No: 0040812604565101 **or** Carmel Cooperative Credit Union Ltd. Bamenda Acc. No: 261 **or** ORANGE Mobile Money: 699902618 **or** MTN Mobile Money: 674495895.

PUBLICATIONS BY CHRISTIAN RESTORATION NETWORK (CRN/PRAYER STORM)

1- Prayer Storm Daily Prayer Guide (monthly devotional)
2- Power Must Change Hands Vol.1: Dealing with Evil Foundations
3- Power Must Change Hands Vol.2: Pursue Overtake and Recover All
4- Power Must Change Hands Vol.3: Jesus Christ Must Reign
5- Power Must Change Hands Vol.4: Arise and Shine
6- Power Must Change Hands Vol.5: Family Restoration 1
7- Power Must Change Hands Vol.6: Family Restoration 2
8- Power Must Change Hands Vol.7: Raise an Altar
9- Power Must Change Hands Vol.8: Commanding Total Victory
10- Power Must Change Hands Vol.9: Enjoying Your Freedom in Christ
11- Power Must Change Hands Vol.10: Supernatural Breakthrough
12- Festival of Fire Series No.1: Let the Fire Fall
13- Festival of Fire Series No.2: Anointed Vessels
14- Festival of Fire Series No.3: God's Agent of Revival
15- Festival of Fire Series No.4: Raising Altars of Restoration
16- Festival of Fire Series No.5: Foundations of a Blessed Family
17- Dominion
18- Divine Overflow
19- Unbreakable
20- Higher Heights

21- Arresting Family Destroyers 1
22- Arresting Family Destroyers 2
23- Praying Like Jesus
24- Conquering the Giant Called Poverty
25- Generous Living
26- Bind the Strongman
27- Personal and Family Deliverance
28- A Difference by Fire
29- Your Time for Divine Expansion
30- Jesus Our Jubilee
31- The Choice of a Friend
32- Christians and Politics
33- A Dynamic Prayer Life
34- Restoring Broken Foundations

NB: Our publications are in English and French.

For copies, contact your local books store or direct your request to:

Prayer Storm Team
P.O. Box 5018 Nkwen, Bamenda
Tel.: (237) 679465717 or 675686005 or 677436964
crnprayerstorm@gmail.com
prayerstorm@christianrestorationnetwork.org

Prayer Storm Online Store:
With MTN or Orange Mobile Money *(for those in Cameroon)* and E-Wallet *(for those abroad)*, you can easily obtain the electronic version of this book and other CRN publications via **www.amazon.com** or via **www.amazon.com** at **https://shorturl.at/pqxyT** or **www.christianrestorationnetwork.org/our-bookstore**. **https://goo.gl/ktf3rT**

Contact (237) 679.46.57.17 or
prayerstorm@christianrestorationnetwork.org

www.ingramcontent.com/pod-product-compliance
Lightning Source LLC
La Vergne TN
LVHW050650100826
845148LV00011B/2061